iConnected

Use AirPlay, iCloud, Apps, and More to Bring Your Apple Devices Together

iConnected

Use AirPlay, iCloud, Apps, and More to Bring Your Apple Devices Together

Ben Harvell

WILEY

iConnected:
Use AirPlay, iCloud, Apps, and More to Bring Your Apple Devices Together

Published by
John Wiley & Sons, Inc.
10475 Crosspoint Boulevard
Indianapolis, IN 46256
www.wiley.com

Published simultaneously in Canada

ISBN: 978-1-118-54374-0

Manufactured in the United States of America

10 9 8 7 6 5 4 3 2 1

For general information on our other products and services or to obtain technical support, please contact our Customer Care Department within the U.S. at (877) 762-2974, outside the U.S. at (317) 572-3993 or fax (317) 572-4002.

Wiley also publishes its books in a variety of electronic formats and by print-on-demand. Some content that appears in standard print versions of this book may not be available in other formats. For more information about Wiley products, visit us at www.wiley.com.

Library of Congress Control Number: 2012955838

Colophon: This book was produced using the ITC Mendoza Roman typeface for the body text, Myriad Pro for the chapter titles, and Syntax for the subheads, sidebar text, and caption text.

Credits

Acquisitions Editor
Aaron Black

Editorial Director
Robyn Siesky

Business Manager
Amy Knies

Senior Marketing Manager
Sandy Smith

Vice President and
Executive Group Publisher
Richard Swadley

Vice President and
Executive Publisher
Barry Pruett

Editor
Carol Person, The Zango Group

Technical Editor
Galen Gruman

Design and Layout
Galen Gruman, The Zango Group

Cover Designer
Michael E. Trent

Copy Editing, Proofreading,
and Indexing
The Zango Group

Acknowledgments

This book has been sitting in my head since I first managed to wire up a network of speakers across my home and stream any audio source to every room. Fortunately, Apple's development of AirPlay has allowed the introduction of a wireless version of that system along with a greatly reduced number of tripping accidents. The iCloud portion came much later, when Apple had finally shook off its less-than-impressive history of bungled online services and introduced a simple yet powerful system that really does keep all your devices in sync.

As always, I ran the idea by Aaron Black at Wiley, who was keen to see the possibilities afforded by AirPlay and iCloud and so allowed me to put it into writing. Thanks to him and all the Wiley staff for making writing these books a pleasure.

Special thanks also go to Galen Gruman and Carol Person who, undeterred by our last outing as a team for *Make Music with Your iPad*, showed the same superhuman levels of patience and professionalism to help get this book into your hands in a legible form.

Finally, to all the developers who not only write great apps but are also happy to answer stupid questions from a guy writing a book — thank you. There are too many of you to name individually but, if you received an e-mail from me in the last year, consider yourself on the list.

About the Author

Ben Harvell is a freelance writer based in Bournemouth, U.K., and a regular contributor to major technology magazines and websites including *Macworld, MacFormat*, and *MacLife*. Formerly the editor of *iCreate Magazine*, Ben has written several consumer technology books with a focus on Apple products such as *Make Music with Your iPad*, also published by Wiley. He blogs at www. benharvell.com, tweets at @benharvell, and provides a professional copywriting service for mobile app developers at www.pocket-copy. com.

To Mum and Dad.
Enjoy the first book I've written that you can actually use and understand ... for the most part.

contents

Chapter 3: Stream Music and Movies across Your Home

Chapter 4: Entertain Yourself from the Couch

Chapter 5: Take, Sync, and Share Photos

Chapter 6: Stay in Touch

Chapter 7: Staying Organized on the Move

Appendix: Apple TV Tips and Tricks

Index   293

intro

A Brief History of Apple Online

SO YOU WANT TO KNOW ABOUT ICLOUD AND AIRPLAY. GOOD, you've come to the right place. I will, however, in my capacity as author and Apple aficionado, first need to take you on a short history of Apple's online and streaming services before we reach the Promised Land that both products embody.

We've come a long way, baby

Yes, I appreciate that you probably want to know how to sync your e-mails or access iTunes purchases from your iPhone. I assure you, we'll get there soon. I simply think it's important that you get a little perspective on iCloud (and a brief mention of the birth of AirPlay) before breaking down their features and usage. If you're really not in the mood for a history lesson, by all means skip to Chapter 1, but I'll do my best to keep things brief while filling you in on the ups and downs of Apple's adventures online. You see, as much as both iCloud and AirPlay look like polished tools these days, things weren't always this way.

The eWorld Debacle

As the word "Internet" became more frequently used and understood by the public in 1994, a partnership between AOL and Apple saw the launch of eWorld. With its colorful graphics and mock town square layout (see Figure I-1), it was a unique route to the web for those struggling to make sense of all this talk of superhighways and megabits, featuring an e-mail client, news reader, and communities (filled with ePeople!). eWorld, without marketing or advertising in a particularly troubling financial period for Apple, was ultimately a failure and the town closed its gates on March 31, 1996. While AOL took up the mantle with its web service and seemingly relentless free trials on CD (you know, the things you used as coasters throughout the late 1990s), Apple still harbored dreams of an online service.

FIGURE I-1

The town square layout of the eWorld interface in 1994

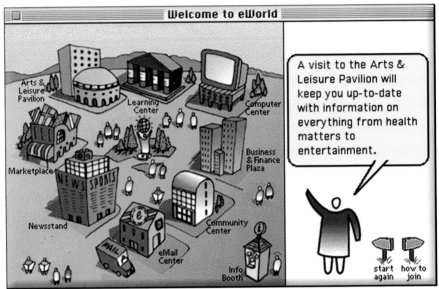

FIGURE I-2

iTools offered new features such as the @mac.com e-mail address

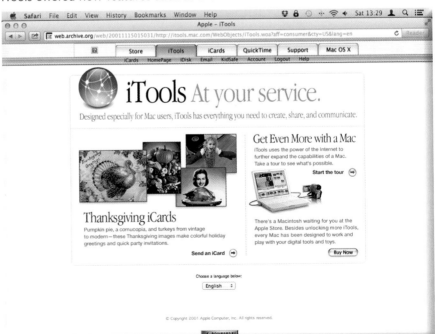

New Beginnings with iTools

By the new millennium, the company had decided that a preceding "i" in a product name was far more trendy than an "e," and it brought iTools (see Figure I-2) to the Mac in January 2000. iTools launched as a free product with four main selling points. First there was KidSafe, a website filter designed to alleviate fears that children would be instantly corrupted after typing three Ws into a web browser. Second, there was Mac.com, the beginning of the famed @mac.com e-mail address. iDisk offered a whopping 20MB of online storage accessed from the desktop, and then there was HomePage, a rudimentary website builder. At the launch of iTools, Steve Jobs, Apple's then CEO, proclaimed "Mac users can now do things on the Internet that Wintel users can only dream of." Later, Apple would update iTools to use WebDAV technology, allowing it to be used outside the Mac platform and developed an iTools application for Windows XP.

The Year of .Mac

It's fair to say that the lure of Apple's iTools and its replacement, .Mac, was chiefly the cachet of an @mac.com e-mail address, more advanced features were in the pipeline, however, as the service began to take the shape of the tools we know today. As Apple's fortunes began to turn in the early 2000s, with consumers looking for an alternative to Windows and the idea of being a Mac user becoming cool again, iTools was renamed .Mac and several new features were introduced, including backup and a virus scanner provided by McAfee. In late 2002, over one hundred thousand users had subscribed to .Mac at the lofty cost of $99.99 per year with a free transition period for iTools users and a discounted rate. Additional features were added during the six-year run of .Mac, including an online photo and video sharing tool, up to 30GB storage (at additional cost), and enhanced e-mail service. During this period, in June 2004, Apple also announced the new AirPort Express base station featuring a protocol called AirTunes for streaming audio across a network. This would, of course, eventually become AirPlay. But now back to the online stuff. ...

It's Not You, It's MobileMe

With the humble, flawed beginnings of eWorld firmly in the past, Apple confidently took its online services to the next level in 2008, launching MobileMe (see Figure I-3) as a replacement to .Mac alongside the new iPhone 3G. Not only were several .Mac features dropped (including iCards, .Mac slides, and .Mac Groups) but the MobileMe service simply didn't perform as advertised, leading to terrible reviews and moaning users. Syncing was a mess, the online platforms buggy, and some users couldn't even access e-mail. The curse of eWorld had returned.

With so many issues plaguing users of MobileMe, Apple offered refunds and even an extension on the original extension of the free MobileMe trial, providing some users with more than three free months of MobileMe use.

FIGURE I-3

The colorful form of Apple's unmitigated online disaster, MobileMe

And Then There Was iCloud

After the surprising failure that was MobileMe, Apple needed new direction and focus for its online service. So it introduced iCloud in June 2011 with the most important new feature versus the beleaguered MobileMe: It was available for free. New users and existing subscribers of the soon-to-be-discontinued MobileMe were welcomed to the new service, which was more geared to syncing and backup for Macs and iOS devices as well as offering the @me.com e-mail address. Which leaves us at a convenient point to begin this book. You might have an iCloud account already, or you may have been scared away by MobileMe and are now tentatively peering at iCloud and its offerings before making the jump. Trust me, things are better. Let's get you up and running with iCloud.

Notes on This Book

Throughout this book, you'll spot several items aimed to help you understand the topics covered or provide additional information.

The first you'll come across are some odd looking boxes that look a little bit like barcodes. These are in fact QR codes, which you can scan with the camera on your iPhone, iPad, or iPod Touch using a QR code reader app to access App Store and iTunes Store links. You can download a QR reader from the App Store to your device (many are free), and I recommend installing one before you continue reading.

Second, there are sidebars toward the end of several chapters called "A Day in the Life." These sidebars offer a rundown of all the topics and processes in a chapter condensed into fictional real-world activities. They show you how the features and techniques described in a chapter will benefit you on an average day as well as provide inspiration on how you might better use iCloud, AirPlay, and Apple's other connected technologies on a day-to-day basis.

Finally, there are symbols used throughout the book for actions you take on a computer.

I use ⌘ to indicate Apple menu (at the far left of the menu bar).

I use several symbols to indicate keys you would use on a computer:

⌘: The Mac's Command key.

⊞: The Windows key on a PC.

⇨: The separator for a menu sequence, so "Edit ⇨ Copy" means to choose Copy from the Edit menu.

Also, I use the + symbol in keyboard shortcuts to indicate keys that should be pressed simultaneously, so ⌘+A means to press and hold ⌘ and then press A before releasing both keys.

1

iCloud
Explained

So what exactly is iCloud? And how do you get it if you don't already have it? I tend to test out consumer products and services via my mom. Yes, seriously. A prime example of this technique was when she asked me whether she needed to sign up to this "iCloud thingy" she had received an e-mail about. As she's a Mac, iPhone, and iPad user, I told her that it would make sense to sign up to iCloud and ran her through the benefits of syncing all her contacts and being able to access her calendar on all her devices. It wasn't until I came to the fact that she would also receive an @me.com e-mail address that she informed me she already had one. She was already using iCloud but didn't realize it.

I'm sure the same is true for many Mac or iOS users, primarily because iCloud is designed to get out of your way and work in the background with little or no upkeep required. An iCloud account can be created on a Mac, a Windows PC, or on an iPhone, iPad, or iPod Touch and it be can surprisingly easy to forget the process and assume that you aren't an iCloud user and that your products "just work" the way that Apple intended. That's what Apple wants and, contrary to my opinion, shouldn't be meddled with for you to achieve the ultimate experience.

That's not strictly the case, however. Truly understanding iCloud rather than blindly letting it "work" is the route to true harmony when using Apple's suite of online services. For example, what happens if, through an accidental click here or there, all your contacts disappear or are pulled from the wrong source? Suddenly, all your devices have the wrong phone numbers (or none at all) with iCloud blissfully unaware, assuming it's still doing a great job. Similarly, not everyone knows exactly what parts of his or her operating system is controlled by iCloud and what isn't. Is iCloud, for example, related to your iTunes account? Can you access your e-mail without it? What about photos? Knowing how iCloud works and how to adjust its settings are therefore important.

Why Do You Need iCloud?

The best way to understand iCloud is to think of it as an invisible cable that runs among all your devices connected to your iCloud account. Every device you own that connects to your iCloud account has its own "cable" that also connects to a server somewhere in Apple's vast data center. Whenever you make a change to information synced via iCloud on any of these devices, that information is sent (along the invisible "cable") direct to the iCloud server that houses your account. iCloud then checks your other devices to see if that change is present on them and, if not, pushes it down the invisible "cable" to all your devices so that everything remains in sync.

The information passing along this invisible "cable" varies in type, depending on the action you perform on your device. For example, if your friend changes his phone number and you add the new number to the Contacts app on your iPad, that change to his contact information is sent to the iCloud server. iCloud notes the change and sends the updated phone number to all the devices connected to your iCloud account. So, the next time you check your iPhone, for example, the new number will be there and ready to use.

This invisible iCloud "cable" also works for photos taken on your iPhone or iPad, music and movies downloaded from iTunes, and apps downloaded from the App Store. With the right syncing settings turned on, the photos will be present on all your devices a few seconds after they are added to your device. If that last passage still seems confusing, have a look at Apple's simple take on the process in Figure 1-1, which uses a photo taken with an iPhone that is sent to the iCloud server before being pushed to the iPad and laptop connected to that account. Got it?

So that's what iCloud actually does when syncing devices, but there's more. To answer the original question, we need to look at iCloud's benefits, which I assume you're starting to appreciate already.

FIGURE 1-1

iCloud receives information and pushes it to all your devices.

SCREEN IMAGES: BEN HARVELL

To clarify (in a nutshell), here are the six major benefits you receive once you're signed up to iCloud:

- **A free mail account, calendar, and address book accessible across all your devices.** If you've tried Gmail or MobileMe (the service iCloud replaces), you know the drill already. These services naturally work with the corresponding apps on your iOS devices and Mac computers as well as being accessible online.

- **Synced App Store and iBookstore purchases.** Every time you buy an app or book on one device, it automatically downloads on your other devices. (Don't worry: You can turn this off if you want to.) You can also access any books or apps you've purchased in the past and download them again for free. This works on all your devices.

- **Simple, wireless backup.** When you charge your iPhone, iPad, or iPod Touch while it is also connected to a Wi-Fi network, all your data, photos, settings, apps, and more are copied to the iCloud servers. You may never need this feature but, should you lose or break your device, simply entering your password allows you to restore your new device from this backup.

- **Storage.** Documents created on an iCloud-connected device using an iCloud-compatible app (these are primarily Apple's apps at the moment) can be accessed on your other devices using iCloud Storage. You get 5GB storage at no cost that is also shared with Mail and any backups you perform; iTunes and photo storage doesn't count against your usage allotment. More storage space can be purchased if required, as I describe later in this chapter.
- **Photo Stream.** Photos taken or imported on any of your iCloud-connected devices are shared with your other devices. Take a photo with your iPhone and it'll be on your iPad when you get home.
- **iTunes in the Cloud.** As with books and apps, your music purchases on one device can be automatically added to your other devices via iCloud if you want. Likewise, you can access previous purchases from iTunes on all your devices. For songs you didn't buy from iTunes, you can use iTunes Match (for a fee); it scans your music collection and matches songs to those in the iTunes Store, allowing you to access them on any of your devices, even if you didn't buy them from iTunes. More on that later, too.

For a free service, that's not a bad deal and, if you own an iPhone and an iPad, an iPad and an iPod Touch, an iPhone and a Mac, or any other combination of these devices, it's beginning to reach the point where you *need* iCloud to make the most of them. Which models of those devices work with iCloud? Read on.

What Hardware and Software Do You Need?

You don't actually need more than one device to use iCloud but, should you have more than one, you'll certainly

iCloud Compatibility

Here's a quick list of the devices that support iCloud:
- iPhone 3G S, 4, 4S, and 5 running iOS 5 or later.
- All iPads running iOS 5 or later.
- Third-generation (late-2010 model) or later iPod Touch running iOS 5 or later.
- Any Mac running OS X 10.7 Lion (with the 10.7.4 or later update installed) or OS X 10.8 Mountain Lion, with iTunes 10.6 or later.
- Any Windows PC running Windows Vista (with Service Pack 2 or later), 7, or 8, with iTunes 10.6 or later and the iCloud control panel.

see more benefit. Devices compatible with iCloud include most recent iPhone, iPad, and iPod Touch models as well as Mac desktop and laptop computers, and Windows PCs. Precise details can be found in the sidebar in this chapter but, if you bought your device in the last couple of years, you're more than likely able to use iCloud. If you're lucky enough to own an Apple TV set-top box as well as any of the other devices mentioned, there are even more iCloud features for you to get your teeth into.

One thing, you need to ensure is that all your devices are running the most recent operating system. You should know how to do this on your desktop and laptop computers but, if not, consult the manual that came with your computer or investigate the most up-to-date version of Windows or Mac OS X compatible with your specific model. If you discover that you can't use iOS 5 or later on your iPhone, iPad, or iPod Touch, OS X Lion or later on a Mac, or Windows Vista or later on a PC, you may encounter trouble. Some iCloud features may be accessible on older operating systems, but it's best to use as recent an operating system as possible. Also, if you're using a Windows PC, you will need Outlook 2007 or later to access iCloud e-mails from your desktop; otherwise, you will be forced to access e-mail through your web browser, which also needs to be up to date.

Do You Need to Buy Storage?

By default, you are provided with 5GB of storage space when you sign up for an iCloud account. This storage isn't quite like other online storage services such as Dropbox or Apple's now-defunct iDisk, because you can't directly access the storage folder. iCloud Storage is simply a space online where documents you save in iCloud-compatible apps, mail data, and backups from your iOS devices are stored and accessed by their respective apps. Other downloads you may make, such as apps, movies, music, and books, as well as shared photos via Photo Stream, are not stored in the same space so you don't have to worry about using up your allocated storage.

The free 5GB allotment should be sufficient for most users, but heavy e-mail use and storing multiple documents in the cloud may begin to fill up your iCloud Storage allowance. My advice is to use the initial amount until you are warned you are nearing your limit. Most people may never receive this warning but if you do, there are other options available. For an additional $20 per year, you can buy an additional 10GB to use on top of your default 5GB (so you get 15GB). For $40

FIGURE 1-2

You can view and manage your iCloud Storage from an iOS device (shown here) or your computer.

per year, you receive an additional 20GB, and for $100 you get a 50GB boost in storage. iCloud Storage can be purchased in the iCloud section of the iOS Settings app (see Figure 1-2), on a Mac via the iCloud system preference, or on a PC via the iCloud control panel. Unless you have a seriously pressing need for more iCloud space and already have an account to upgrade, let's move on to more of the basics. I'll come back to how to upgrade and manage your storage later in the book.

What Is an Apple ID?

Chances are that you already have an Apple ID. If you've ever made a purchase through iTunes, you have an Apple ID, for example. If you have an e-mail address ending in @mac. com or @me.com, you also have an Apple ID. The Apple ID is the e-mail address and password you use to login to all Apple services, and it's best to use the Apple ID associated with your iTunes account with iCloud as well. You do have the option to use a separate account for iTunes and iCloud if you want (I explore that in Chapter 2), but it makes things a lot simpler if you stick with one ID for everything.

One of the few reasons you may want to use one Apple ID for iTunes purchases and another for iCloud is to preserve previous iTunes purchases you made on iTunes and to be able to access them on all your devices while still creating an @me.com address. However, if you have those purchases downloaded to your computer, you could use iTunes Match (see Chapter 3) to add them to your new iCloud account at a later stage.

Another reason is security: If someone got a hold of your iCloud account ID, he or she would also be able to purchase things at the iTunes Store, App Store, and in some cases even the Apple Store using the same account. Keeping them separate limits the risk of having your sign-in information stolen.

You may also share an Apple ID with a family member but want to use a personal iCloud account for your e-mail and other iCloud contents. If that's the case, there's a method for that too that I explore in Chapter 2.

For the cleanest possible route to using iCloud, it's best to start with a fresh account. It's also the easiest way to follow the setup process: Simply pick your own @me.com e-mail address and you're good to go. So let's figure out if you have an iCloud account already.

Do You Already Have iCloud?

It's simple enough to forget that you created an iCloud account when you first set up your iOS device or even switched from a MobileMe account when iCloud launched. Fortunately, it's easy to check whether iCloud is currently running or if you have created an iCloud account.

For iPhone, iPad, and iPod Touch users:

1. Tap the Settings app icon on your device's Home screen to open the Settings app.

2. Scroll the list of settings to the iCloud label and tap it to open the iCloud pane, shown in Figure 1-3.

3. If there is an e-mail address listed in the Account field, you have iCloud running on your device.

FIGURE 1-3

You can check whether you have an iCloud account setup via your device's Settings app.

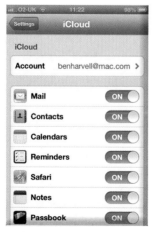

For Mac users:

1. Choose ➪ System Preferences or click the System Preferences icon in your Dock to open the System Preferences application.

2. Click iCloud in the System Preferences app window to open the iCloud system preference (shown in Figure 1-4).

3. If your name appears below the iCloud logo and a list of services are shown on the right of the pane, your computer is connected to iCloud. Click your name to show the e-mail account used for iCloud.

For PC users:

1. In Windows Vista and 7, choose Start ➪ Control Panel to open the Control Panel application, then click the iCloud icon to open the iCloud control panel. In Windows 8, press ⊞+X to open the Power User menu, choose Control Panel to open the Control Panel app, and click the iCloud icon to open the iCloud control panel. (Sorry, but you can't run iCloud on a Windows RT device.) If your PC doesn't have the iCloud control panel, you can install it from Apple's website at www.icloud.com/icloudcontrolpanel.

FIGURE 1-4

Mac users can check their iCloud account in System Preferences.

2. If your name and e-mail address are listed in the iCloud control panel, you have an iCloud account linked to your computer.

If iCloud doesn't appear to be running on your computer or iOS device, you can run through a couple more checks to make sure you didn't create an account at any stage. First, search all your e-mail accounts for any confirmation of an iCloud account creation from Apple. Finally, visit www.icloud.com and enter the e-mail address and password you are most likely to have used with iCloud. If you still come up with nothing, it's safe to say that you're unlikely to have an iCloud account running.

If that's the case, step right this way to set one up.

Set Up iCloud on All Your Devices

There are several ways to set up a new iCloud account, be it on a brand-new iOS device, an existing device, or on a Mac. PC users are required to set up iCloud on an iOS device or a Mac first, before adding the account to their PC using the iCloud control panel. Once you have set up iCloud on one device, you can simply add that account to your other devices without going through the setup process again. Choose one of the options below to create an iCloud account.

On a new iOS device

When you first turn on a brand-new iOS device, you have the option to set up an iCloud account as you go. This option appears as part of the iOS setup process, and you can also log in to an existing iCloud account if you want.

1. Turn on your new iOS device and swipe across the screen to begin the installation process. Follow the steps until you reach the Set Up screen in the next step.

2. Select the set up options (Set Up as New iPhone or Set Up as New iPad is probably best for most users) and tap the Next button.

FIGURE 1-5

You can create an Apple ID and iCloud account when setting up an iOS device.

3. Tap the Create a Free Apple ID button (shown in Figure 1-5).

4. Use the selection wheel at the bottom of the screen to select your birthday, then tap the Next button.

5. Enter your first name and last name in the fields that appear, then tap the Next button.

6. The next screen allows you to use a current e-mail address or get a free iCloud e-mail address. You can also change an existing e-mail address if required. Tap Get a Free iCloud Email Address and then tap Next.

7. Enter the first part of the e-mail address you want to use (before the @ symbol) and tap Next. Tap Create on the alert window that appears if you're happy with your e-mail address.

8. Enter a new password for your account and verify it in the second field, then tap the Next button.

9. Select a security question and answer, then tap the Next button.

10. Agree to the terms and conditions document by tapping the Agree button. Your new Apple ID is now created.

FIGURE 1-6

iCloud is automatically enabled when you create an account during iOS setup.

11. Tap the Use iCloud button to enable iCloud on this device (see Figure 1-6). Tap the Next button to continue.

12. Select whether you want to back up your device to iCloud or to your computer by tapping the corresponding button, then tap the Next button.

13. Select whether to use Find My iPhone by tapping the corresponding button. Tap the Next button. Select whether to use Siri (on devices that support it) by tapping the corresponding button followed by the Next button. Do the same for Diagnostics & Usage on the next screen.

14. Tap Start Using iPhone or Start Using iPad to complete the setup process.

15. By default, all iCloud services will be turned on using the e-mail address you entered during setup. You can check this by launching the Settings app and tapping the iCloud option.

On an existing iOS device

You can add an iCloud account to an iOS device you are already using:

1. Tap the Settings app icon on your device's Home screen to launch the Settings app.
2. Scroll to the iCloud label and tap on it to open the iCloud pane.
3. Tap the Get a Free Apple ID button at the bottom of the screen. To create a new iCloud account, follow the steps in the preceding "On a new iOS device" section, starting with Step 4. If you want to add an existing account, enter your iCloud account e-mail address and password, then tap the Sign In button.

On a Mac

Setting up an iCloud account on a Mac requires OS X 10.7.4 Lion or later and is done in the System Preferences application.

1. Choose ➪ System Preferences or click the System Preferences icon in your Dock to open the System Preferences application.
2. Click iCloud in the System Preferences app window to open the iCloud system preference.
3. If you have an iCloud account already, enter your e-mail address and password in the provided fields, then click the Sign In button. If not, click the Create an Apple ID link at the bottom of the pane.
4. Enter your location and birthday details using the pop-up menus, then click the Next button.
5. To use an existing e-mail address, select the Use an Existing Email Address radio button. To create a free iCloud e-mail address, select the Get a Free iCloud Email Address radio button. Now enter the e-mail address you want to use as well as your name, password, and Secret Question details. Click the Next button.

FIGURE 1-7

Setting up iCloud in Mac OS X's System Preferences application

6. Accept the iCloud terms and conditions by checking the box at the bottom of the pane. Then click the Continue button.

7. Check the boxes next to the services you want to use with iCloud (shown in Figure 1-7), then click the Next button.

Add an iCloud account to a Windows PC

Setting up iCloud on a PC requires Windows Vista (with Service Pack 2 or later), Windows 7, or Windows 8. (The Windows RT operating system used in some tablets does not support iCloud.) You also need the iCloud control panel for Windows to complete the iCloud setup process. You also need to have created an iCloud account on a Mac or iOS device before you can add an iCloud account to a PC via the iCloud control panel.

1. Using your computer's web browser, go to www.icloud.com/icloudcontrolpanel to download and install the iCloud control panel for Windows.

2. In Windows Vista and 7, choose Start ➪ Control Panel to open the Control Panel application, then click

the iCloud icon to open the iCloud control panel. In Windows 8, press ⊞+X to open the Power User menu, choose Control Panel to open the Control Panel app, and click the iCloud icon to open the iCloud control panel.

3. To add an existing iCloud account, enter your Apple ID and password and click the Sign In button.

Add an iCloud account to an Apple TV

The Apple TV, which I cover later in the book, can also access your iCloud account so you can access your Photo Stream as well as media purchases from the iTunes Store.

1. Turn on your Apple TV and navigate to the Settings screen.
2. Choose iTunes Store.
3. Choose Sign In.
4. Enter your iCloud e-mail address, then click the Submit button. Enter your password, then click the Submit button.

You can have several Apple IDs associated to an Apple TV. To add additional IDs, follow the previous steps but for Step 2, choose Accounts and then choose Add New Account. Switch among IDs (only one can be active at a time) using the Switch to Account list after you select Accounts.

What Is AirPlay?

Now that you have all that iCloud business set up, it's time to look at AirPlay for the second part of this introduction and installation process.

Fortunately, AirPlay doesn't require quite the explanation or compatibility requirements of iCloud, primarily because the protocol really does just one thing: stream media between devices. AirPlay devices come in the form of wireless speakers and, of course, the Apple TV, shown in Figure 1-8. You can also buy hi-fi systems with a built-in AirPlay receiver if you have the money to spare.

With any of these devices in your home, you can wirelessly stream media, photos, videos, and music, to your chosen device from a Mac or iOS device, and even play certain games for the iPhone, iPod Touch, and iPad over AirPlay on your Apple TV.

The video component of AirPlay is currently restricted solely to streaming to the Apple TV, but the audio option is far more flexible, with a wide range of speakers and docks available.

Setup is as simple as powering up a device and selecting it from the AirPlay pop-over on your iOS device in most situations or from iTunes on your Mac or PC.

What hardware and software do you need?

To use AirPlay, you need a compatible host device and a compatible receiver. This could be a Mac and an Apple TV or an iOS device and an AirPlay-compatible speaker. Ideally, you'll want all the above and maybe a few more speakers for a complete wireless setup. Alternatively, for audio-only streaming, you can also transmit from a Mac or iOS device to an Apple AirPort Express base station connected by an audio cable to a speaker or hi-fi system.

FIGURE 1-8

The third-generation Apple TV

GALEN GRUMAN

You need to ensure that your iOS device or Mac is running the most recent software it can handle. For streaming audio and video from apps on the iPhone, iPad, and iPod Touch, you need iOS 4.3 or later; on a Mac, you need iTunes 10.2 or later. Pretty much any Mac running OS X 10.5 Leopard or later can stream audio or video via AirPlay in iTunes, as can pretty much any PC running Windows XP Service Pack 2 or later, Windows Vista Service Pack 2 or later, Windows 7, or Windows 8 (but not Windows RT). For iOS devices, you can use any iPad, the iPhone 3G S or later, and the second-generation (2010 model) or later iPod Touch. Your Apple TV also needs to be the second-generation model or later (that is, one of the black models) and be running Apple TV software version 5.1 or later.

To mirror your iPad's display to a TV or projector via an Apple TV using what Apple calls AirPlay mirroring, you need an iPad 2 or later model (that is, any iPad except the very first model). For an iPhone, you need an iPhone 4S or 5. To mirror a Mac's display, you need a Mac with the appropriate video chip running OS X 10.8 Mountain Lion — that limits you essentially to Macs released in 2011 or later. (You can't mirror a Windows PC's display.) For mirroring, your devices need to be connected to the Wi-Fi network via the 802.11a, 802.11g, or 802.11n protocols — not the old 802.11b protocol; most routers from the last four years support at least one of the required protocols.

Set up an AirPlay network

The final, crucial piece of the AirPlay puzzle is a wireless network. AirPlay operates over Wi-Fi and requires all your devices to be connected to the same network to function. Your iOS devices connect to the network via Wi-Fi (make sure they're connected by going to the Wi-Fi pane in the Settings app), while your Apple TV and Macs can use either Wi-Fi or wired Ethernet — as long as the Wi-Fi network and Ethernet network are connected to each other, such as through a

USE SIRI TO GET MORE INFORMATION

Siri has learned a few new tricks since it was originally launched on the iPhone in 2010. (When this book went to press, Siri was available on the iPhone 4S and 5 and on the third-generation iPad, fourth-generation iPad, and iPad Mini when connected to the Internet.) You can now ask Siri questions about sports scores, teams, movie screenings, and more. Siri will respond with up-to-date information related to your query. For example, you can say "What were the football scores at the weekend?" and Siri will pull up the soccer or NFL scores depending on your location. You can then drill down and ask for information on specific players or league standings by asking questions like "Who is winning the NFC East?"

Similarly, asking "What's on at the movies?" will have Siri provide information on show times at the nearest cinema to your current location. The movies will also be shown in order of popularity based on reviews at Rotten Tomatoes.

Controlling music playback via voice commands isn't a new feature in iOS, nor is asking Siri which track is currently playing. But you can now also use Siri to launch apps for you. Telling Siri to "Open Calendar" switches you to the Calendar app on your iOS device. And you can get details from many apps. For example, you could ask, "What does my day look like?" and have Siri list the number of appointments in your Calendar for that day.

common router or wireless routers connected to a wired router or broadband gateway. Chances are that your home network is already set up in a way that works.

AirPlay speakers differ by model as to how they are set up. Some require a connection to a computer via USB cable, others require an Ethernet or Wi-Fi connection to a computer, and some provide an iOS app that allows set up via Wi-Fi from an iPad, iPhone, or iPod Touch. Consult your device's instructions to connect it to your network. You connect an Apple TV to your Wi-Fi network via its Settings menu.

Where Is the AirPlay Button?

Once all your devices are connected to your network, the speakers and Apple TV units (as well as any AirPort Express base stations you may be using) will appear on the list of available AirPlay devices when you tap or click the AirPlay button (⬆) on an iOS device or a Mac.

So where is that AirPlay button? It resides in apps like iTunes on a computer and in a variety of apps on iOS devices, such as Podcasts, Videos, Phone, Music, Public Radio, and YouTube. (In these apps, it also lets you access any paired Bluetooth devices for audio streaming, such as a car stereo or headset.)

You can also access the AirPlay button from the multitasking dock in iOS: Double-press the Home button to reveal this dock at the bottom of the screen, then scroll to the left to see the AirPlay icon. If your device supports AirPlay mirroring, you'll see the Mirroring switch after you tap the AirPlay button. On a Mac that supports AirPlay mirroring, you should see the AirPlay icon in the menu bar at the top of the screen.

2

Access Your Music and Movies on All Your Devices

ITUNES AND ICLOUD WORK TOGETHER TO PROVIDE A SEAMLESS purchasing experience across all your connected devices and is one of the biggest selling points for the service. Apple loves to promote the "music anywhere" message — and for good reason. Once you get used to having access to all your iTunes media on all your devices, you'll wonder how you ever lived without it.

Whether you are downloading movies, TV shows, music, or podcasts, iCloud helps you keep all your purchases in sync and available across Macs, PCs, and iOS devices. This means that purchases made on one iCloud device can be set to automatically appear on the others so you don't have to go through the download process multiple times. You also have the option to download previous purchases from your iTunes account on any device connected to your iCloud account.

Beyond that, the extra-cost iTunes Match service allows you to use these services with music you didn't buy from iTunes by scanning your iTunes library for songs you ripped from a CD or downloaded from another source online and matching them to songs in the iTunes catalog.

Download Your Previous iTunes Purchases on Any iCloud Device

You know that feeling when you've filled your iPod Touch, iPad, or iPhone with music, movies, and podcasts, only to think of a song, film, or show you wish you'd included? With iTunes in the Cloud, that situation should become a thing of the past, assuming you have access to the Internet. Any purchase you made through iTunes, the App Store, or the iBookstore can be downloaded again for free from any of your devices connected to your iCloud account.

The process differs slightly on each device, so I outline the exact details in this section.

Download previous music, movie, and TV purchases

Previously purchased music, movies, and TV shows can be accessed using the iTunes app on an iOS device and via iTunes on a Mac or PC. The iTunes apps on iPhone and iPod Touch differ a little from the iPad version, so I've included instructions for both.

No matter what device you are using, make sure you are signed in to your iTunes account to access your previous purchases. On a Mac or PC, do so by choosing Store ⇨ Sign In. On an iOS device, go to the iTunes & App Store pane in the Settings app and enter your Apple ID and Password, then tap Sign In.

On the iPhone and iPod Touch:

1. Tap the iTunes icon on your device's Home screen to launch the iTunes app.
2. Tap the More button at the bottom of the screen.
3. Tap Purchased in the list that appears.
4. Tap Music, Films, or TV Series from the list that appears, depending on what you want to download.
5. A list of your previous purchases appears (see Figure 2-1). You can search these categories or show only purchases that aren't on your device already by tapping the appropriate tabs at the top of the screen.
6. When you find the item you want to download, tap the Download button (⬇). Or tap the Download All button to download all items not on your device.

On the iPad:

1. Tap the iTunes icon on your iPad's Home screen to launch the iTunes app.
2. Tap the Purchased button at the bottom of the iTunes screen.
3. Select the type of media you are looking for (Music, Films, or TV Series) by tapping one of the tabs at the top of the screen.
4. A list of your previous purchases is shown (see Figure 2-2). You can search these categories or show only

FIGURE 2-1

Previous purchases in the iTunes app on iPhone and iPod Touch are hidden in the More section.

FIGURE 2-2

The iTunes app for the iPad offers tabs to search for previous purchases.

purchases that aren't on your device already by tapping the tabs at the top of the screen.

5. When you find the item you want to download, tap the Download button (⬇). Or tap the Download All button to download all items not on your device.

In iTunes 11 (Mac or PC):

1. Click the iTunes Store button to open the iTunes Store window.

2. If it's not already selected, click the Home button (🏠) at the top of the iTunes Store window.

3. Click Purchased from the Quick Links section at the top right of the screen.

4. Select one of the tabs at the top of the screen that appears to choose a media type, such as Music, Movies, or TV Shows.

FIGURE 2-3

The Search Purchased Items field in iTunes offers a quick route to downloading previous purchases.

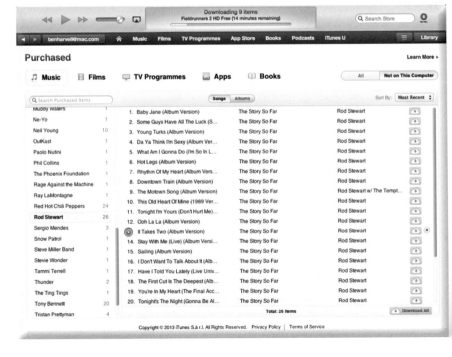

5. You can now search for content you have purchased by name, using the Search Purchased Items field (not the Search Store field) or by clicking the Not on This Computer tab to show only items that aren't present in your iTunes library (see Figure 2-3).

Download previous iBooks purchases

The process for downloading previously purchased books via the iBookstore is the same for the iPhone, iPod Touch, and iPad versions of the iBooks apps. To download iBooks purchases on a Mac or a PC, follow the preceding steps for previous iTunes purchases, but go to the Books pane in Step 4.

1. Tap the iBooks icon on your device's Home screen to launch the iBooks app.
2. Tap the Store button at the top of the iBooks screen.
3. Tap the Purchased button at the bottom of the screen.
4. Your previous purchases are now listed (as shown in Figure 2-4) and you can sort them by tapping the All

FIGURE 2-4

The iBooks app allows previous book purchases to be downloaded on iOS devices.

or Not on This iPad/iPhone/iPod tabs at the top of the screen.

5. To download a previously purchased book, tap the Download button (▣) next to the book's title.

In iBooks 3, released in October 2012, you can also just switch to the Purchased Books view in the iBooks library (using the Collections button at the top of the screen) and then tap any book cover with the iCloud icon in its upper right corner to download it.

Download previously purchased apps

Apps you've bought but are not on your iOS device can be downloaded through the App Store app. The iPad version and the iPhone and iPod Touch versions of the App Store differ slightly, so I cover both methods for downloading previous app purchases. To download previously purchased apps in iTunes on a Mac or a PC, use the same steps as for music, movies, and TV shows explained earlier but select Apps in Step 4.

On an iPhone or iPod Touch:

1. Tap the App Store icon on your device's Home screen to launch the App Store app.

2. Tap the Updates button at the bottom of the App Store app's screen.

3. Tap Purchased on the screen that appears.

4. Your previous App Store purchases are listed (see Figure 2-5) with the most recent downloads at the top of the list. Tap the Not on This iPhone/iPod tab at the top of the screen to view apps that aren't currently installed on your device.

5. Tap the Download button (▣) to download an app.

On an iPad:

1. Tap the App Store icon on your iPad's Home screen to launch the App Store app.

2. Tap the Purchased button at the bottom of the App Store screen.

FIGURE 2-5

Apps you have purchased previously can be downloaded again from the App Store app.

FIGURE 2-6

Tapping the Not on This iPad tab shows previous app purchases that aren't currently installed.

3. Your previous App Store purchases are shown on the screen (see Figure 2-6). Tap the Not on This iPad tab to show only apps that aren't currently installed on your iPad.
4. Tap the Download button (⬇) to download an app.

Download podcasts

For podcasts in iTunes on your Mac or PC, be sure you are in the Library window (tap the Library button at the upper right if not). Select Podcasts from the Media pop-up menu at the upper left, then select the desired podcast from the list at left, click the Refresh button (↻) to check for new episodes, and click the Download button (⬇) that appears to the right of any nondownloaded episodes.

For podcasts on an iOS device, open the Podcasts app, select the desired podcast from the list, and then tap the Download button (⬇) next to any desired episode that has not yet been downloaded. To have podcasts sync automatically, go to the Settings app's Podcasts pane and be sure the Sync Subscriptions and Auto-Downloads switches are set to On.

Download iTunes U courses

For iTunes U courses, open the course in iTunes on your PC or Mac, then expand the course's materials by clicking the disclosure triangle to the left of its name. Course materials available for download have the Download button (⬇) to their left. (New courses added will sync with your iOS devices the next time you sync via iTunes.)

On an iOS device, open the iTunes U app, tap the course you want to download materials for and tap the Download (⬇) button next to each undownloaded item, you want. To have course materials sync automatically, go to the Settings app's iTunes U pane and be sure the Sync Courses and Notes switch is set to On.

Turn on Automatic iTunes Downloads

The Automatic Downloads feature uses iCloud to detect when a song, app, or book is downloaded on one of your devices and then automatically downloads the same content on your other iCloud-connected devices. With this setting turned on, you can happily download content and be safe knowing that it'll be waiting for you when you access another of your devices.

For example, let's say you hear a song on the radio when you wake up one morning and download it from the iTunes app on your iPad. On the way to work, you fancy hearing it again, so you pop in your iPhone headphones, access the Music app, and there's your song. The same is true of books you might be reading on your iPad or games you're playing: If you download them on your iPad, both will be available on your iPhone or iPod Touch if you want a quick distraction on your lunch break.

Use the Settings app's iTunes & App Stores pane on iOS devices to enable Automatic Downloads, as Figure 2-7 shows. You can separately enable the Music, Apps, and Books switches. (Apps and books that aren't compatible with a particular device will not be automatically downloaded, such as an iPad app on an iPhone or an iPad Multi-Touch book on an iPhone.)

Automatic Downloads can also be turned on in iTunes on a Mac and PC, as Figure 2-8 shows: Open the Preferences dialog box by choosing iTunes ➪ Preferences on a Mac or Edit ➪ Preferences in Windows, go to the Store pane, and then check the types of media to automatically download via the Music, Apps, and Books check boxes.

You may have Automatic Downloads enabled only in some devices, or perhaps automatically download only some types of media on some devices. Such customization can be useful if you're running low on space on one device.

On iOS devices, the Automatic Downloads works using Wi-Fi and cellular connections, but you may want to disable the cellular option to avoid using the monthly data allowance allocated by

FIGURE 2-7

Selecting whether to automatically download music, apps, and books on an iPad

FIGURE 2-8

Setting Automatic Download preferences in iTunes

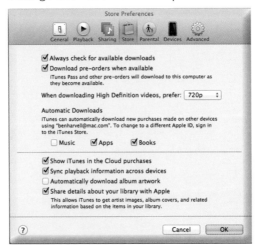

your carrier. Do so by setting the Use Cellular Data switch to Off in the Settings app's iTunes & App Stores pane.

Sync iTunes Store Previews with iCloud

iOS 6 brought some nice enhancements to song previews in iTunes. When you're visiting the iTunes store via the iTunes app, you can now continue to listen to a song preview while you browse to other areas of the store rather than have the music be cut off as soon as you navigate away from the song or album you were looking at.

Even more useful is the ability to access a list of songs you have previewed on iTunes, regardless of the device you were using. To access this neat feature, simply tap the History button (▤) that appears at the top right of the iTunes app's screen. (You also get this button in the iTunes Store window on your Mac or PC when running iTunes 11.) A list appears of each song you've previewed (see Figure 2-9), organized by date, and you can opt to view the item again or purchase it

---

FIGURE 2-9

View songs you've previewed in the iTunes app on any device.

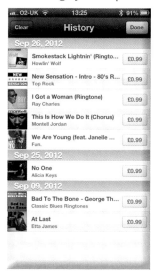

directly from this list. Of course, you need to be signed in to your iTunes account for this feature to work.

Use iTunes Match

iTunes Match (shown in Figure 2-10) is a little hard to get your head around at first. Perhaps that's because it actually offers the too-good-to-be-true matching service it claims. For a mere $25 annual subscription, iTunes Match scans all the songs in your iTunes music library (yes, even those ripped from your friend's CD collection or downloaded from another store) and determines whether they match a song available in the iTunes Store.

All the songs from your library that are matched become available to all your devices via iCloud at full 256Kbps AAC quality (that's nice and clear for those unfamiliar with the jargon). So, in effect, iTunes Match not only lets you make

FIGURE 2-10

The iTunes Match window in iTunes

legal those ripped and even pirated songs in your library for a fraction of their original cost, but it also improves the quality of those hissy tracks you may own. That's not a bad deal for an annual subscription that costs less than a couple of albums. Even better, you get to keep those higher-quality versions even if you don't renew your iTunes Match subscription.

Songs that can't be matched are uploaded to iCloud in their original form so you can access them on all your devices, too. They do, however, take a while to transfer, so it's a good idea to clean up your iTunes library before you sign up to iTunes Match.

Make the most of iTunes Match

If you want the move to iTunes Match to be as clean and efficient as possible, there are several steps to take to get yourself prepared.

Get your house in order

Organizing your iTunes library will make for a simpler route to iTunes Match perfection. By adding the correct information to music in your library, iTunes Match will be able to match them to songs in the iTunes Store more quickly, with the added bonus that you will be able to figure out which songs have been matched and which haven't without having to guess at a track name or album. iTunes Match also looks at the length of a track to determine whether it's a match for an equivalent song in the iTunes Store, so a difference of a few seconds here or there could mean a better-quality version of a song isn't available through iTunes Match.

Although you could go through each song in your library and make changes manually, it's best to enlist the help of specialist software, especially if you have a very large music collection. On a Mac, Equinux's Song Genie is a good option for an overall tidy, adding missing information to songs names and tags. It also works alongside its sister app

FIGURE 2-11

TuneUp (at right) cleans iTunes libraries, and removes, duplicates, and adds cover art.

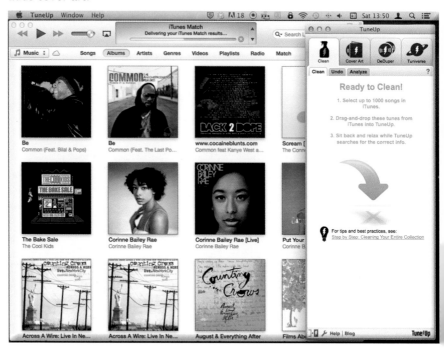

CoverScout to apply missing album artwork. Another option is TuneUp, by TuneUp Media (see Figure 2-11), which offers many of the same features as Song Genie plus the option to remove duplicate tracks that, again, slow down the matching process. It also saved me around 8GB on my hard drive by killing those pesky songs that appear multiple times for one reason or another.

Both Song Genie and TuneUp use smart song recognition technology to analyze the actual waveforms of a song rather than go by the name of the track or album, and they are definitely worth investing in before using iTunes Match or if you simply want a cleaner music library.

Trim the fat

In the same vein as the preceding section, the more you tidy up your iTunes library, the faster iTunes Match can match your songs. Deleting songs from your library and getting rid of duplicates will not only save space on your hard drive but also reduce the time iTunes Match takes during setup.

TuneUp does a good job removing duplicates but, if you want to take the manual approach, you can choose View ⇨ Show Duplicate Items in iTunes to show songs that appear more than once in your library. You might be surprised by just how many they are. Remove the duplicates, get rid of any dud files and unwanted tracks that may have appeared in your collection over the years, and all should be well.

A useful way to find songs to delete from your iTunes library is to sort them by time when viewing your entire

THE BENEFITS OF CLEANING YOUR ITUNES LIBRARY

Joe Frabotta of TuneUp Media explains how cleaning up your music before using iTunes Match can save a lot of time and effort:

"One limitation with iTunes Match is that it doesn't always do a great job matching every song. iTunes Match sometimes will have trouble finding the right information for each song as it copies it to the iCloud. This is usually an issue of metadata. iTunes — whether on your desktop or portable device — relies on metadata to organize and display music. Each song in your library contains *metatags*, which are small amounts of data that provide more information about the file such as song name, artist, album, genre, date released, and so on. If your metadata is disorganized, iTunes will be as well. Unless you just started building your library or have used TuneUp before, you probably have plenty of problems with your tags — missing song names, iterations of the same artist (The Beatles; The Beetles; Beatles, The), duplicates of songs (Don't Let Me Down; don't let me down), albums without cover art, and even some songs without any information at all!"

library as a list. Shorter songs tend to be MP3s added by mistake or incomplete songs that should be removed. Just watch for short tracks that feature as intros to an album. For other sorting methods, you can add a new column type to the list view by right-clicking or Control+clicking any of the column titles and selecting a column option from the list that appears.

Burn your books

Well, don't actually burn them but make sure that iTunes Match doesn't pick them up for scanning. Audiobooks are big files and aren't necessarily always marked as audiobooks but as music. To stop iTunes Match from wasting time uploading them to iCloud, select all the audiobooks in your library and press ⌘+I on a Mac or Ctrl+I on a PC to edit their info. In the Options pane of the dialog box that appears, select Audiobook from the Media Kind pop-up menu. Of course, you might want your audiobooks to be uploaded to iCloud, in which case, leave them be or, if you can handle not having them in your iTunes library, save them somewhere else on your computer and remove them from iTunes before starting iTunes Match.

Get cheaper, better quality music

Now here's a cunning plan and one that's perfectly legitimate thanks to the subscription fee you pay for iTunes Match each year. It's a simple technique but one you might not have thought of. Here goes: The next time you want to buy music, don't buy it from the iTunes Store. That's right. It might sound odd but, if you can buy the same music cheaper from another source, do it. Thanks to iTunes Match, that same music can be added to your iCloud library but you don't have to have bought it at the full iTunes price to access it on all your devices. So, first check the price of the song or album you want to buy on iTunes and then shop around the other online music stores.

Amazon.com and Google Music usually have good deals, and there are many more options out there. Likewise, if you can pick up a copy of an album on CD for cheaper than the iTunes price, do it. You can then rip the disc to your iTunes library and add it to your iCloud library. Similarly, if you can find music that's cheaper but at a lower bit rate (quality) than you're used to, don't be put off. When added to iTunes Match, you'll automatically receive the 256Kbps-quality AAC versions from iCloud. Of course, if you are going to buy your music elsewhere, it's best to make sure it's available in the iTunes Store too or it will have to be uploaded to iCloud, not matched.

Take the cautious approach

If you're not prepared to sit and wait while iTunes Match goes through thousands of the songs in your library, there is another option. This is also a good tip for anyone with an iTunes library with more than 25,000 songs, the limit you can store using iTunes Match.

All you need to do is to create a new, clean iTunes library to sit alongside your existing, everyday library. Start by selecting the songs from your original iTunes library that you want to use with iTunes Match, and drag them out of iTunes and into a folder somewhere on your computer. Now close iTunes and launch it again while holding the Option key (Mac) or the Shift key (PC). A window appears asking you to select the library you want to use as well as the option to create a new one. Click Create Library and call it something memorable like iTunes Match. You now have a blank iTunes library to play with, and you can simply drag the folder of music you created earlier into this library to use it with iTunes Match. To avoid confusion, uncheck the Copy Files to iTunes Media Folder option in iTunes' Preferences dialog box's Advanced pane.

Subscribe to iTunes Match on a Mac or PC

Followed all the tips from before? Got $25 to spare? Then you're ready to set up iTunes Match.

First make sure you have the most recent copy of the iTunes software installed on your computer. Visit www.itunes.com to check. In iTunes:

1. If you're not signed in to your iTunes Store account, choose Store ⇨ Sign In, then enter your username and password in the dialog box that appears, and click Sign In.

2. Choose Store ⇨ Turn On iTunes Match.

3. Click the Subscribe button (or Add This Computer if you have used iTunes Match on a different computer) in the window that appears and enter your password

FIGURE 2-12

iTunes Match scans your iTunes library and uploads songs it can't find a match for.

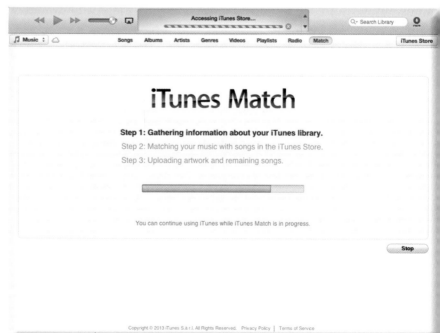

to confirm. Then click the Subscribe button in the same window.

4. iTunes Match then performs three steps to scan and match songs in your library as well as upload artwork and unmatched songs (shown in Figure 2-12).

It's best to leave iTunes Match running while it completes the matching process, but you can click the Stop button to pause the process. Simply click the button again to restart the process.

Access your music through iTunes Match

Once you have run the iTunes Match setup process, accessing music on your iOS devices is relatively simple. You first need to turn on iTunes Match on all the devices you want to use it with and then simply access the songs from the Music app as you would music stored locally on your device.

1. Tap the Settings icon on your device's Home screen to launch the Settings app.

FIGURE 2-13

iTunes Match needs to be switched on to be accessed from an iOS device, then it can download your music library list.

A DAY IN THE LIFE: ICLOUD MUSIC AND MOVIES

So let's imagine you wake up one morning and grab your iPad. You've received an e-mail from one of your favorite app developers telling you about a brand-new app. You download the app to your iPad and have a quick play with it before taking a shower.

On your way in to work you decide to listen to some music but remember that you haven't synced your iPhone recently to add any new music. Fortunately, you've run iTunes Match on your computer so you launch the Music app on your iPhone and access the album you wanted to listen to via iCloud.

While you listen, you decide you want to use the new app you downloaded to your iPad. Thanks to Automatic Downloads, the app is also on your iPhone so you can use it right away.

On your way home, you browse the iTunes Store on your iPhone to pick out an album to listen to while you make dinner. You preview a few songs before you arrive home and grab your iPad on your way to the kitchen. By accessing the Preview History list in the iTunes app, you can view the songs you previewed on your iPhone and choose one to download and listen to.

As you go to bed and plug your iPhone into your alarm clock dock, you fall asleep listening to your new album purchase that has automatically downloaded to your iPhone.

2. Scroll the list and tap the iTunes & App Stores label to open the iTunes & App Stores pane.

3. Set the iTunes Match switch to the On position.

4. Press the Home button to exit the Settings app and then tap the Music icon to launch the Music app.

5. The Music app now connects to iTunes Match and, after a brief period (see Figure 2-13), shows the songs

available to you. A cloud icon next to a song or album indicates one not stored on your device.

6. Tap a song title to play it. Any song stored in iCloud is downloaded to your device as it plays, so it doesn't have to be downloaded again on that device.

TIP: If you decide you don't want a song stored on your device any longer, swipe to the left over its name in the songs list and then tap the Delete button that appears. The song is still available via iCloud but is no longer stored on that device.

3

Stream Music and Movies across Your Home

BEFORE AIRPLAY AND OTHER STREAMING TECHNOLOGIES CAME about, you really only had two options for streaming music across your home. (Movies didn't figure in at all.) The first option was to buy a ridiculously expensive wireless system that required using a compatible base unit to send the audio and a set of receivers dotted around your house. The second option was to run audio cables from a TV or hi-fi system between rooms and manually connect them to speakers. Both options were time-consuming, restrictive, and definitely not future-proof.

Although you might be able to add new speakers using both methods, people using a wireless home entertainment solution needed to buy the same brand of speaker to match their system, normally at a premium price. People with a wired solution had to add more unsightly cables and again buy more speakers to add to their setup. Both options also offer limited control, normally only allowing audio from one source — a TV, stereo, or radio, for example. They're the sort of systems built into expensive houses in the 1980s and 1990s, more often than not fixed into walls and fittings, slowly becoming obsolete with no option to upgrade without a hefty electronic and maintenance bill.

The AirPlay Alternative

But now there's AirPlay, doing away with almost all these issues while adding amazing flexibility, control, and a range of prices to suit your budget. The additional ability to stream video should make the decision to use AirPlay a no-brainer.

How you set up your AirPlay network can range from the basics, such as using just an iOS device and an Apple TV to fantasy-level installations with an AirPlay speaker in every room connecting to your iPhone, iPad, and iPod Touch.

All you really need to get started, however, is a wireless network, an iOS device, and an AirPlay-compatible receiver, so you're looking at around a tenth of the outlay compared to a dedicated system. From an initial simple setup you are, of course, free to add more speakers and other AirPlay devices as you want rather than be forced to choose from a limited range of expensive additions offered by just the manufacturer of your existing kit.

It took a little while to catch on, but there are now hundreds of AirPlay-compatible speakers on the market with prices to suit all budgets. Some of them are wired speakers that require wall-outlet power, others are powered by batteries. And there are models that include a dock for your iPhone, iPod Touch, or iPad, which only increases their usefulness. A handful of stereo manufacturers have even built AirPlay technology into their hi-fi systems so, as well as enjoying TV, games, and Blu-ray through your home entertainment system, you can also stream music from your iOS devices or computers for the ultimate connected experience.

Are You AirPlay-Ready Already?

If you bought an AirPlay-compatible speaker, you probably already know the situation, but those not au courant with all this wireless stuff might not realize that you already own the requisite technology to use AirPlay. Let's break this down into sections.

1. A wireless (Wi-Fi) network is essential for AirPlay. Got one of those set up? You've passed the first test. Move on to Step 2. For anyone without a wireless network, come join us in the 21st century: It can cost you less than a pair of movie tickets to pick up a decent wireless router.

2. Do you have a computer running iTunes, an iPhone, iPad, and/or iPod Touch? Assuming they're fairly recent models and are using the latest software (see Chapter 1), you're in.

3. And where do you want to stream? The next step is sending video or audio from your devices to a compatible receiver. This could be an Apple TV, an

AirPlay-compatible speaker system, or an Apple AirPort Express base station. You can hook up any speaker with an audio-in jack (normally marked as AUX or A/V In) to one of these devices (bar AirPlay speakers, of course) using a simple mini (3.5mm) audio cable that you can get in most electronics and even hardware stores for next to nothing.

If you fit all three of the criteria, hey presto!, you're ready to set up your first AirPlay network. If you didn't quite get 100 percent on the test, it's not going to cost you that much to get in the game.

What Do You Want AirPlay to Do for You?

Now comes the important part: deciding how best to use AirPlay to suit your needs. Planning at this stage is important and allows you to accommodate any unexpected hiccups, including the range of your wireless network and equipment you may need to buy. The devices you currently own will likely dictate your choices.

For example, if you have an iMac in the bedroom or office and an Apple TV in the living room, you can use AirPlay to access music and movies from your iMac's iTunes library and photos from your iMac's iPhoto on your TV, but you won't have the option to stream music to multiple rooms until you add speakers to your network.

Likewise, if you have an iPad and an AirPlay speaker, you will be able only to stream audio to that speaker from your iPad. You'll need an Apple TV to handle the iPad's video content.

You get the idea. The key is knowing what you want and how you go about getting it, so think about what excites you about AirPlay and how much money you have to spend, and all should be well and good.

The dream AirPlay setup

If money is no object and you're looking for the ultimate solution, buy an AirPlay speaker for each room in your home (of course, if money is indeed no object, your home is likely to be enormous, so this step in itself could cost a pretty penny!). That covers the audio streaming angle.

There are AirPlay speakers available that won't break the bank as well as a bunch that will set you back about as much as a new laptop. One of my personal favorites is the $449 Libratone Zipp, which is colorful, portable, and battery-powered, so you can place it in any room. Another great option, if money is no object, is the $600 Bowers & Wilkins Zepellin Air, which looks as good as it sounds and will happily fill a large room with sound. iHome's $300 iW1 and $200 iW2 AirPlay speakers are affordable and compact enough to slot in any space in your home or office. Bowers and Wilkins also offers smaller but still high-fidelity AirPlay speakers in the form of its A5 ($750) and A7 ($985) speakers. These speakers don't come cheap, but if you're after the best quality from an AirPlay speaker, you'll be hard pressed to find a better option.

If you can't find a place for an AirPlay speaker in your bathroom, you might want to invest in the iShower, a waterproof Bluetooth speaker that allows you to control music playback while you wash. It's also handy by the pool or on the beach.

You then need to buy an HDTV for each room you want to send video to, again assuming money is no object. Each HDTV needs its own Apple TV to act as an AirPlay receiver. (Scratch the second trust fund for your least favorite kid!) Now you need to control this monster network of AirPlay kit, so it's time to invest in iOS devices and computers. You'll probably want a MacBook or PC equivalent so you can stream audio to any of the speakers dotted about your abode and mirror your screen to any of the HDTVs connected to an Apple TV. The same goes for the iMac or desktop PC in your office.

When you're casually strolling through your palatial atrium or visiting the north wing where grandma does her pilates, you'll want to be able to control your whole system, so an iPhone, iPod Touch, or iPad running Apple's Remote app (which, as much as you may hate the idea of low cost, is free) is the next solution. While you're at it, why not get a similar device for each member of the family?

Finally, you may find that in the outer reaches of your campus-like home, the Wi-Fi signal for your iOS devices isn't available. Why? Because a standard wireless router or AirPort base station can only transmit up to around 300 feet, and that's on a good day. To maintain a constant Wi-Fi signal throughout your home, you'll need to extend the existing network with additional base stations or any of the numerous Wi-Fi range extenders on the market such as those from Netgear and Cisco Systems.

And then you're done. You have a complete AirPlay setup across your home. Just don't tell your accountant.

The more realistic AirPlay setup

Now back to the real world. Chances are you have a less grandiose vision for your AirPlay network: the ability to listen to music in different rooms and stream videos and other media to your TV from your iOS devices or computer. Not only is this plan inexpensive, but it's the one AirPlay was designed for.

Start by thinking about which rooms you would like to stream music to and then set up and position your speakers accordingly. Remember, if you have an AirPort Express base station, it can double as a wireless speaker in your network by attaching a standard speaker to it via an audio cable. If you have more than one AirPort Express knocking around, you have the added bonus of using one to provide the wireless network (and act as a speaker) and the other to extend that network elsewhere in your home while also acting as a speaker.

With your speakers in place, decide where you will primarily use your Apple TV. Do you want to stream video to your TV in the bedroom or access movies on your computer through your living room TV? Of course, at the Apple TV's $99 cost it's realistic to buy two Apple TVs to cover both TVs, but I'll leave that decision up to you.

Test Your AirPlay Network

With all your AirPlay devices in place and connected to the network, perform a quick test using an iOS device or a laptop.

If you need help connecting your AirPlay speakers, consult the manual that came with your device. Many speakers offer an iOS app to help with setup while others need to be connected directly to your router or computer via Ethernet during installation.

Connect your iOS device or laptop to your wireless network and move to the speaker or Apple TV furthest from your router. Head to the Wi-Fi section in the Settings app on an iOS device or turn on Wi-Fi on your laptop if it isn't on already and look for wireless hotspots. If your main wireless router can be detected, you shouldn't have any problems connecting to your AirPlay devices.

If you can't find your wireless router on the list of available networks, your next step is to extend your Wi-Fi router's range. Most electronics stores offer Wi-Fi range extenders for minimal cost but, if you have a spare AirPort base station or a wireless router with range-extending features, you can quickly extend the range of your existing network to cover the Wi-Fi blank spots. The free AirPort Utility software for iOS, Mac, or Windows is required to use an AirPort base station as a range extender; for other routers, you'll have to read the manual for your router to learn how to use it as an extender, also called a bridge. (Usually, all you need to do is turn off DHCP on the extended router via its

FIGURE 3-1

Test your AirPlay network by using the multitasking dock's iOS AirPlay button () to select a speaker, then play music or other audio.

settings, which are usually accessible via a web browser.) The methods all differ but it shouldn't be too tricky to perform.

TIP: Of course, if you can move your router to a new location so its signal covers your whole home (somewhere in the middle, ideally), you can save a little time and money.

Once everything is in range and set up according to the instructions for each device, you can make sure all your AirPlay devices are available by double-tapping the Home button on your iOS device to open the multitasking dock and then scrolling to the left until you see playback controls and the AirPlay button (see Figure 3-1). Tap the AirPlay button () to show all available AirPlay devices, and make sure all your speakers and other devices are available.

To perform the same test on a Mac or PC, launch iTunes and begin playing some music from your iTunes library. Now click the AirPlay button ([▲]) at the upper left right of the window, next to the playback controls (as you can see later in Figure 3-6), to show all your available AirPlay devices. If you have a Mac that supports AirPlay mirroring, click the AirPlay icon ([▲]) in the menu bar to get a list of available Apple TVs.

Stream Music and Other Audio

Now that your speakers, Apple TVs, or AirPort Express base stations are set up and ready to receive tunes, it's time to figure out the best way to use them. This will, naturally, depend on the devices you want to use, be it an iOS device, a Mac, or a PC, and whether you're streaming to an AirPlay speaker, Apple TV, or an AirPort Express connected to a speaker or hi-fi system. Whatever scenario you go for, it's not too difficult to get your music streaming the way you want it.

Before you begin, make sure that the speakers you want to stream to are switched on and ready to receive audio. Likewise, make sure your Apple TV is on and the TV or speakers connected to it are also switched on. If you are streaming to an AirPort Express base station, make sure it is plugged in, the status light is green, and your speakers are attached to it with an audio cable and that they are also switched on.

Stream audio from your iOS device via AirPlay

While you probably want to stream audio from an app like Music or Podcasts on your iPhone, iPad, or iPod Touch, you can also send all your iOS device's audio to an AirPlay receiver. You won't hear system sounds like e-mail alerts over AirPlay, but any sound generated by apps you run or music you play will be sent to the connected AirPlay device. This approach can be handy if the app you are using doesn't offer its own AirPlay output option or if you are switching among a bunch of apps and want the audio to continually stream to your AirPlay speakers.

It's worth noting that there is a slight delay in streaming audio via AirPlay, often more than three seconds thanks to high-tech goings-on between your device and the speaker, so using apps that require the sound to be as immediate as possible (such as music apps or games, for example) might not be ideal.

Also, AirPlay lets you stream to just one speaker at a time. If you want to stream your iOS device's audio to multiple AirPlay speakers, there is a workaround using Airfoil described later in this chapter. And the Remote app, also covered later, lets you play to multiple speakers from a computer's iTunes library.

FIGURE 3-2

The AirPlay button () is normally found near the playback controls of an app (here, at their upper right, in black because it's not turned on)

Stream audio from iOS apps

If you want to stream audio from an app on your iPhone, iPad, or iPod Touch, you first need to make sure your app supports AirPlay streaming. (If not, use the multitasking dock's AirPlay control instead.) The AirPlay button (⬚) normally appears near the volume control for an app, as Figure 3-2 shows, or in its settings pop-over and allows you to select the device you want to stream audio to.

AirPlay is most frequently used in audio apps such as Spotify and NPR but more and more apps are using the feature. For example fitness apps may provide AirPlay support for personal training, so you can work out while listening to instructions via a speaker, or cooking apps might use audio to explain recipe steps.

Use the Remote app to control streaming music

Apple's free Remote app for iOS devices is arguably one of the most important tools for AirPlay users. Not only does it provide a way to control streaming to all your AirPlay devices, it allows you to stream to multiple speakers at once, accessing media from iTunes on your computer or controlling an Apple TV.

To use the Remote app, you first need to add your iTunes library to it by enabling Home Sharing in iTunes, at which point the library will appear in the Remote app. You can then select any content stored in your iTunes library and stream it to any of your AirPlay devices. On your computer's iTunes, choose File ➪ Home Sharing ➪ Turn on Home Sharing, then enter the username and password for the computer whose iTunes you want to be the master library for AirPlay — create an account via that menu option on your current computer if it will be the AirPlay master. On an iOS device, sign in to Home Sharing in the Settings app's Music or Videos pane — it doesn't matter which.

FIGURE 3-3

The Remote app on an iPad accessing an iTunes library via Home Sharing

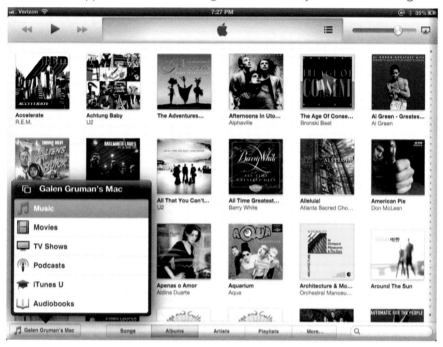

Download and install the Remote app from the App Store. It's free! Then launch the Remote app and select the desired iTunes library from the list. (You may see only one library listed if you are only using one computer with Home Sharing.)

As Figure 3-3 shows, when viewing a Home Sharing library, Remote's interface looks much like iTunes on a computer and allows you to search for music and movies without being at your Mac or PC. You can even create Genius playlists in the Remote app that are then stored in iTunes on your computer. The app works with all iOS devices connected to your network, which means you can use it on your iPhone, iPad, and iPod Touch. You can even use it across devices, because Remote stays in sync with other devices running Remote on the same Home Sharing account, so you can begin playing music on your iPhone and make changes in another room using your iPad.

Available AirPlay devices are shown when the Remote app's AirPlay
button () is tapped.

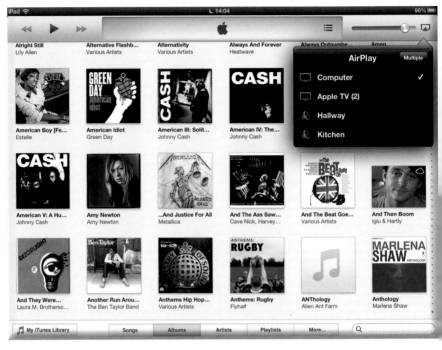

Stream music from iTunes with the Remote App

When it comes to using the Remote app, it couldn't be simpler. Just make sure your device is connected to the same network as your computer and AirPlay speakers and that iTunes is running on the computer on which the iTunes library you are using is stored. From there you are free to pick your songs, pick a speaker (see Figure 3-4), and then play songs, albums, or playlists to stream audio to your heart's content.

Stream to multiple AirPlay devices from the Remote app

As well as streaming audio to any AirPlay device, the Remote app offers the additional benefit of streaming to

FIGURE 3-5

Tapping the Multiple button in the Remote app's AirPlay devices list (the button's name then changes to Single) allows multiple speakers to be selected and have their volumes independently controlled.

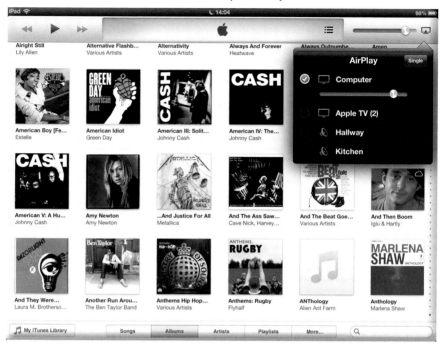

multiple AirPlay devices at once, with a volume control for each speaker.

Tap the Multiple button at the top of the list of AirPlay devices, then select each device to enable. A volume bar appears under each selected device, as Figure 3-5 shows, which you can adjust as desired. (Tap the Single button to restrict Remote to just one selected device.)

The support for multiple devices is ideal when you're hosting a party to provide music to all your guests or for more mundane tasks like housework when you are moving from room to room. The Remote app can stream all types of audio to multiple speakers, including audiobooks and podcasts, so you will never miss a second of your audio as you walk around your house.

Stream Audio from iTunes

iTunes on a computer allows you to stream audio to a single AirPlay speaker or to multiple ones if required, by selecting the available devices via the AirPlay button ( ) at the top of the window.

If the AirPlay button ( ) doesn't appear when you launch iTunes, make sure you have the most recent version of the software (available from www.itunes.com) and that your computer is connected to the same network as the AirPlay speakers (or Apple TVs) you want to use. Windows PC users often have trouble with AirPlay and, if so, should try disabling their firewall or antivirus software temporarily or reinstalling the Bonjour software that installs with iTunes for Windows (get it from www.apple.com/support/bonjour).

When you are streaming via AirPlay, it's best to use a higher volume setting in iTunes than on the speaker itself to achieve the best sound. This doesn't mean whacking the volume up to full and playing music at potentially speaker-damaging, if not ear drum-damaging, levels. As a general rule, you'll reduce hiss from the speaker by turning down the speaker's output rather than forcing it to amplify a quiet source.

1. Make sure your computer is connected to the same network as the AirPlay speakers you want to use via Wi-Fi or Ethernet connection.

2. Launch iTunes and choose the library type whose audio you want to play (Music, Movies, TV Shows, Podcasts, iTunes U, or Tones) from the Source pop-up menu at the upper left of the iTunes window (the menu has no name, but will name the current library, such as Music).

3. Click the AirPlay button ( ) at the upper left of the window (to the right of the playback controls) to open a pop-over listing the available AirPlay speakers.

4. Select the AirPlay speaker you want to stream your music to from the list that appears (see Figure 3-6).

FIGURE 3-6

After selecting a source library in iTunes, use the AirPlay pop-over to select AirPlay speakers.

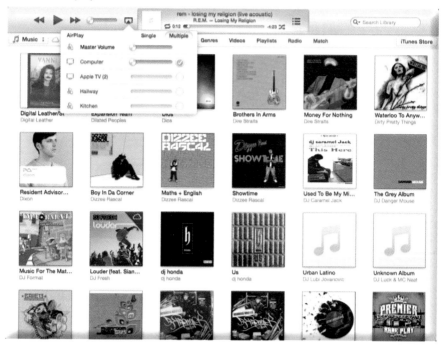

5. Start playing your music or other content through iTunes.

6. Use the volume slider in the playback controls to set the level of the audio sent to the speaker. You may also be able to control the volume on the speaker itself.

When you open the pop-over of AirPlay sources in iTunes, notice the Multiple button at top (see Figure 3-6). It works like the Multiple button in the iOS Remote app: Click it, then select the speakers and other AirPlay devices you want to send the audio to. You can set the volume for each AirPlay device separately with the slider that appears below each selected device.

Click the Single button to send the audio to just one AirPlay device, or simply deselect all but one device to send the audio to just that one.

Stream Audio from Other Apps

It's all well and good to stream music from iTunes to your AirPlay devices, but what about audio from other apps on your computer? If you use a Mac running OS X Mountain Lion, you can stream sounds from any application via AirPlay. Otherwise, you can use the Airfoil software, which has the added benefit of supporting multiple AirPlay speakers.

Stream audio from your Mac

To use an AirPlay device as your Mac's audio output, make sure your computer is connected to the same network as the AirPlay device you want to use. You also need to be running OS X 10.8 Mountain Lion to access this feature.

Bear in mind that this method sends *all* your system audio to the AirPlay device so, unless you want your party songs interrupted by e-mail alerts, IM messages, or other system sounds, quit as many apps as possible before you start sharing your music over AirPlay. The benefit of streaming all your system audio is that you are free to use any app to send audio to your AirPlay device: iTunes for one song, YouTube for another, and Spotify or Rdio for others.

1. Launch the System Preferences application (click its icon in the Dock or choose ⇨ System Preferences).
2. Click the Sound icon in the System Preferences pane to open the Sound system preference.
3. Go to the Output pane.
4. Scroll to the AirPlay device you want (see Figure 3-7). In the Type column next to the selected device, you should see the word "AirPlay."
5. Select the device you want to use.
6. Set the output volume and balance using the sliders below the output device list.
7. Close System Preferences.
8. Launch the app to stream audio from, set its volume level if required, and begin playing the audio you want to stream to your AirPlay speaker.

FIGURE 3-7

Setting the Mac's system audio to stream to an AirPlay speaker

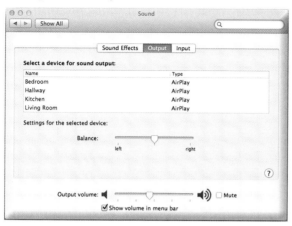

TIP: You can adjust the Mac's audio volume using the Sound icon in the menu bar. If it doesn't display, open the Sound system preference and check the Show Volume in Menu Bar option.

Stream audio from a computer to AirPlay devices via Airfoil

So, we've established that you can stream audio from your computer using iTunes, even to multiple AirPlay devices, and Mac OS X Mountain Lion users can stream system audio to a single AirPlay speaker. But what about Windows PC users and Mac users who don't have or can't run OS X Mountain Lion?

The answer is to use the $25 Airfoil software from Rogue Amoeba (shown in Figure 3-8). This simple app, available for both Macs and PCs, allows users to stream audio from any app on your computer (or all your system audio) to compatible devices, including AirPlay speakers. There's a free trial version you can use to see if you like Airfoil as much as I do.

Once installed, the software is incredibly simple to use. Any AirPlay devices on your network should be available to it automatically. Each AirPlay device has its own volume

FIGURE 3-8

Airfoil can stream audio from any app on your computer via AirPlay.

control setting, so you can set the volume for each AirPlay device from your computer or by using the Reemote app (no, not Apple's Remote app) on your iOS device, which I'll get to later.

There are four very important reasons for using Airfoil to stream to AirPlay devices over iTunes or the audio out setting on a Mac:

1. You can stream to multiple speakers.
2. You can stream audio from apps other than iTunes but not have to send all your system audio to the AirPlay speaker as well.
3. Airfoil is compatible with a wider range of devices than simply AirPlay ones, and it even offers a method to stream audio to your iOS devices — in effect, using them as their AirPlay speaker. This capability reduces the cost of buying more AirPlay equipment if you attach your iOS device to a docking station or speaker system and stream audio to it with Airfoil.
4. You can stream audio from other sources, such as radios, that you connect to your computer.

FIGURE 3-9

Selecting a source application in Airfoil

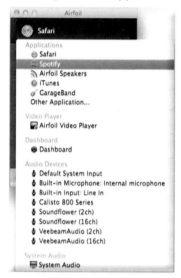

Using Airfoil is easy:

1. If your computer is connected to the correct network and your AirPlay devices are switched on, they should all appear in a list in Airfoil.

2. Click the unnamed button at the top of the Airfoil window (it displays the name of an application such as Safari) and choose the application you want to use to stream audio from the menu that appears (see Figure 3-9). If the application you want isn't listed, choose Other Application and browse for the app you want to use.

3. Select each AirPlay device you want to stream audio to via the buttons to the right of each name. Selected devices are highlighted in blue. To also play the computer's system audio (such as alert tones), choose Computer.

4. Adjust the volume level for each AirPlay device using the slider next to its name.

5. To fine-tune your audio output, click the Mixer button at the bottom right of the window to display the Effects dialog box. Adjust the audio settings as desired and close the dialog box.

6. Begin playing audio from the app you chose. If all is working correctly, the audio should stream, after a brief delay, to all the AirPlay devices you selected.

Use a computer or mobile device as an AirPlay speaker

If you are limited by the number of AirPlay speakers in your home or you don't have any, there is another way to get involved in the AirPlay party. The brilliant developers of Airfoil have created a free little app called Airfoil Speakers (see Figure 3-10) that can turn a Mac, a Windows PC, a Linux PC, an iOS device, or an Android device into an AirPlay speaker. You must be running Airfoil on your computer for Airfoil Speakers to work. Figure 3-10 shows an iPad receiving audio from a Mac via Airfoil Speakers.

Being able to turn an existing device into an AirPlay receiver enhances your options for audio streaming and extends your network of wireless receivers by attaching your computers or mobile devices to speakers or using their built-in speakers.

The app also offers clever tricks like sharing metadata, so if you're using a compatible app like Spotify, for example, the track name and album artwork appear on your device, too. Another brilliant feature is the ability for Airfoil Speakers to run in the background on your device, so you can use other apps while receiving audio from Airfoil. Thus, on an iOS device, you can use Airfoil to stream audio from iTunes on your computer to Airfoil Speakers on your device while still using the Remote app to control playback remotely.

FIGURE 3-10

Airfoil Speakers receiving audio on an iPad from Airfoil on a Mac

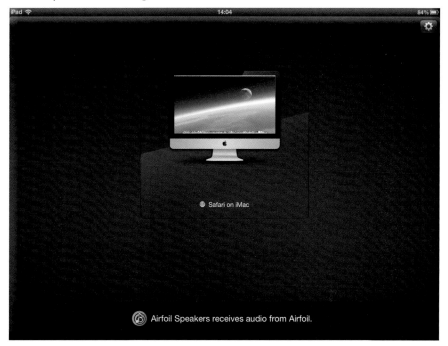

Using Airfoil Speakers is easy:

1. Run the Airfoil Speakers app on the device or computer you want to have act as an AirPlay speaker.
2. On your computer, run Airfoil and select the desired device or computer from the list of available receivers, as Figure 3-11 shows.

FIGURE 3-11

A selected device in the Airfoil app

3. Also on your computer, choose the app you want to stream from or choose the Computer option to send system audio from your computer to the device running Airfoil Speakers.

One of the major drawbacks of AirPlay on iOS devices is its limitation of streaming to a single AirPlay speaker. If, however, you take my advice and buy a copy of Airfoil, you can stream audio from an iOS device back to your computer and then from there to as many AirPlay devices as you want. For example, you can access music from iTunes on your iOS device as well as playlists from streaming music services like Spotify and Rdio.

However, this technique works only for music, audiobooks, and podcasts because there is a four-second delay before the audio reaches the AirPlay speakers — this audio delay would make a video unwatchable. This delay is due to the audio being delayed by around two seconds to your computer and then another two seconds to the AirPlay speakers.

1. Launch both Airfoil and Airfoil Speakers on your computer.
2. On the iOS device you're streaming from, launch the app whose audio you want to stream.
3. Tap the AirPlay button ( ) in that app to choose the computer running Airfoil Speakers and Airfoil from the list of devices. If the app doesn't have an AirPlay button, use the AirPlay control in the multitasking dock instead.
4. Begin playing the audio you want to stream.
5. On the computer that the audio is streaming to, use Airfoil to send that audio to available AirPlay devices, as described earlier in this chapter.
6. In the Airfoil app on your computer, choose Input ⇨ Airfoil to stream the audio from your iOS device that Airfoil Speakers is receiving.
7. The audio from your iOS device will now play to all the AirPlay speakers you selected in Airfoil.

Stream audio from TVs, radios, and other analog devices via a computer

If you use Airfoil, you can connect other audio sources to your computer to stream their audio to your AirPlay speakers. This technique is particularly close to my heart as it includes three of my favorite things: food, sports, and technology.

The idea came to me when I hosted a Super Bowl party and found myself constantly leaving the TV to cook food, get more drinks, or answer the door — I was frustrated that I was missing the pre-game show and then the game itself. So, being the geek, I hooked up the audio from my TV to a computer and streamed that audio via AirPlay to the kitchen and hallway so I didn't miss a play (albeit delayed by a few seconds). While sports might not be your thing, this technique is still very handy. For example, if you're listening to the radio, an iPod, cassette player, CD player, or record player, you could send its audio to all your AirPlay devices.

In most instances, you need to connect a mini (3.5mm) audio cable (the same connection that an iPod's headphones use) to run from your source (a TV, radio, and so on) to the line-in port on your computer. Look for a headphone symbol or a phrase like Audio Out near the audio jack on the source device. Some devices use a composite audio cable (one white plug and one red plug that go into the device); for these, you would use a composite-to-mini audio cable to connect to your computer's line-in jack. The jacks are usually colored red and white, and may be labeled A/V Out or Ext Out.

Obviously, you need a computer near your device for this technique to work — or a very long audio cable. If you can't easily move the audio device (such as a TV) near your computer, use a laptop that you can bring close to the device.

Once you have connected your audio cable to the line-in jack on your computer, run Airfoil on the computer to receive the audio from your device and stream it to your AirPlay speakers. In Airfoil's Input menu, choose the option for your computer's audio-in jack. It may be called Built-In Input, Line In, or something else — you may need to experiment with different choices if it's not obvious. You'll know when you have the right option as you'll see the equalizer at the bottom of the window begin to move, letting you know that audio is being passed into Airfoil via the input you selected. Now, choose the AirPlay speakers you want to stream audio to. If everything is set up correctly, you should hear the audio from your source playing through your AirPlay speakers.

Stream audio from TVs, radios, and other analog devices via an iOS device

So, what if you can't move your computer close enough to your audio source or move the audio source close to your computer? You could connect the analog device to your iOS device instead, and stream from it to an AirPlay device. It sounds simple, doesn't it? Well, it is actually quite complicated! But if you have no other option, take a deep breath and read on.

You'll connect the audio cable from the audio source to your iOS device's audio jack, instead of to your computer's line-in jack. Physically, that's easy. But iOS doesn't know that you want to send audio *in* to your device so you'll need an app to receive the audio and a piece of kit that makes your device think it's being sent audio from a microphone or guitar.

Readers of my book *Make Music with Your iPad* are familiar with 1K Multimedia's iRig and the AmpKit Link. These little devices allow sound to be fed into an iOS device and, with the right software and an Apple TV, you can stream analog input to an iOS device and out again.

So, to use an iOS device as the waystation between an analog audio source and your computer's Airfoil application, you'll need a device like the iRig or AmpKit Link to your iOS device, which would run an audio-input app such as Otreus's StudioMini. You'll also need a mini-to-¼-inch jack adapter to connect the audio cable to the iRig or AmpKit Link.

1. Connect an audio cable between the audio source and the iRig or AmpKit Link. You'll need an adapter to

GET YOUR VIDEO READY FOR STREAMING

If you download all your movies and podcasts from the iTunes Store, you may as well stop reading this section. Its video is perfectly formatted to work with your iPhone, iPad, iPod Touch, and Apple TV as well as iTunes on your computer, so you have nothing to worry about.

However if, like me, you download video from different locations online, rip DVD movies, or import footage from a camcorder, you're likely to run into problems when playing your movies and streaming them over AirPlay. The issue is file format: iTunes requires MPEG-4 files (with the filename extensions .m4v or .mp4) or Apple QuickTime files (.mov). Many people have Window video files (.avi), which need to first be converted to a compatible format for iTunes to be able to import them.

My favorite tool for the job is Elgato's Turbo.264 HD software and USB device (www.elgato.com), which speeds the video conversion by using that USB device to assist your computer's processor. The software can convert multiple video formats and offers handy presets for iOS devices and the Apple TV. Slower but cheaper alternatives are HandBrake (http://handbrake.fr), ffmpegX (www.ffmpegx.com), and Prism (www.nchsoftware.com).

For commercial DVDs you purchase, as well as homemade DVDs from friends and family, the free HandBrake software easily creates iTunes-compatible video files that you then import into iTunes, where they can be played or synced to your iOS devices. Just remember that commercial DVDs you own and rip into your computer may be played back only for your personal use on your devices, not given to others or used for public performances.

connect the mini cable to the iRig's or AmpKit Link's ¼-inch jack.

2. Connect the iRig or AmpKit Link to your iOS device's audio jack.

3. Begin playing audio from your source device.

4. Launch an audio-in app on your iOS device, such as StudioMini. Make sure the app is set to receive input from the headphone jack.

5. Make sure your AirPlay device (Apple TV or speaker) is switched on.

6. Double-press your iOS device's Home button to open the multitasking dock, then scroll to the left until you see the AirPlay button (⬛).

7. Tap the AirPlay button (⬛) and choose your desired AirPlay device from the pop-over that appears — you can't send the audio to multiple speakers.

If all went according to plan, your audio should now be playing through the AirPlay device.

Control Airfoil streaming on an iOS device with Reemote

Although I'm sure you appreciate the benefits of combining Airfoil and Airfoil Speakers with your AirPlay network by now, it does have one drawback: the lack of a way to control the software when you're away from your main computer.

Fortunately, a beautiful third-party app is available for your iOS devices that will help you do just that. It's called Reemote for Airfoil (see Figure 3-12).

    To control Airfoil on your computer with Reemote, you need to install Reemote Server, which is available only for Macs (at www.reemoteapp.com). If you own a Mac, however, it couldn't be simpler to control your Airfoil streaming than with Reemote. From the iOS app, you can access Airfoil on your computer from anywhere in your home, choose which app to stream from, and choose

FIGURE 3-12

The beautiful Reemote for Airfoil app

which speakers to stream to. Brilliantly, several apps —
including Spotify, iTunes, Pandora, Rdio, and Last.fm — can
be controlled from Reemote, so you can play and pause audio
and skip tracks.

If you're a Mac user, I highly recommend the $5 Reemote
for Airfoil for the iOS device you use most frequently. It
really completes your AirPlay and Airfoil setup. If you're a
Windows PC user, check out the section on remote controls
in Chapter 9.

Stream Video via AirPlay

There are many ways to stream audio with AirPlay, but
fewer ways to stream video (and the audio that goes with it).
The most common uses of AirPlay and video (in fact, the only
official methods) are between an iOS device and an Apple
TV and between iTunes on a Mac or PC and an Apple TV.
The Apple TV of course must be connected to a TV for you to
watch the streamed video.

ANDROID AND AIRPLAY

If you've been reading through this chapter and wondering when I'll mention your Galaxy Note or HTC smartphone, my apologies. You probably noticed by now that AirPlay does its best to ward off non-Apple devices through a fairly locked-down network (aside from speakers, of course) but there are small chinks in its armor for Android users to exploit.

Android users should take a look at AirSync (www. doubletwist.com), which streams audio and video in the DoubleTwist app (which can sync to iTunes on your computer) on your Android device via AirPlay. It does work, though not reliably — its AirPlay button often disappears, for example.

where the AirPlay button (⬛) appears. On an iPad 2 or later, or on an iPhone 4S or later, you can mirror the entire screen via AirPlay as well to an Apple TV. You can also stream video from iTunes on your Mac or Windows PC using its AirPlay button (⬛). You can stream your Mac's screen to an Apple TV if you have a compatible Mac running OS X Mountain Lion — a great way to get Amazon Instant Video, Netflix, YouTube, website, or other video streams onto your TV.

There are, however, other methods to stream video via AirPlay if you are using a PC or incompatible Mac or if you don't have an Apple TV; I describe these later in this chapter.

Stream video stored on an iOS device to an Apple TV

The default video streaming via AirPlay from an iPhone, iPad, or iPod Touch involves a fairly locked-down system that requires key parts of the Apple ecosystem to function. Beyond your iOS device, you also need an Apple TV and video content from the iTunes Store or content that has been properly converted to an iTunes-compatible format. Once in iTunes, you can play it via an Apple TV directly from iTunes on your computer, or you can sync it to your iOS device and play it from the Videos app there.

Once you have video content stored on your device and are ready to stream it to an Apple TV make sure your iOS device and Apple TV are connected to the same network and that the Apple TV is switched on. At this point you're ready to send video to your Apple TV.

To play videos from your iOS device's Videos app:

1. Select the movie you want to watch and tap the Play button (▶) to start playback.

2. Next to the playback controls that appear (you may need to tap the screen to show them), tap the AirPlay button (⊡) and choose your Apple TV from the pop-over that appears (see Figure 3-13).

FIGURE 3-13

Streaming video stored on an iOS device

3. The iOS device's screen will turn gray and the video will display on the TV connected to your Apple TV. You can still control the playback and adjust the video's position on your iPad.

4. To return to viewing the video on your iOS device, tap the AirPlay button ( ) again and choose your device from the list.

Stream web video from an iOS device to an Apple TV

Some websites with embedded video content allow you to stream video to your Apple TV, and it is becoming more common for the AirPlay button ( ) to appear when viewing video on the web from an iOS device. Sometimes, you need to view the video in full screen to access the AirPlay button ( ). Once you see the AirPlay button ( ) on a video on a website, simply tap it and choose your Apple TV to begin streaming (see Figure 3-14).

Stream video from an iOS app to an Apple TV

Just as more websites are providing an AirPlay button for their videos when accessed from an iOS device, so too are more iOS apps providing an AirPlay button for their videos. Historically, video apps such as Hulu Plus from the TV networks and cable channels have avoided making it easy to stream their videos to an Apple TV, perhaps because they worry that users of the app may like the experience so much that they eschew traditional television altogether.

In recent years, however, these networks and services have become more confident about the future of television and on-demand viewing, so that little AirPlay button is slowly creeping into more and more video apps. The Netflix and PBS apps in the U.S. support AirPlay, for example. In the U.K., Sky and my personal favorite, NFL GamePass, support AirPlay in their apps (see Figure 3-15).

FIGURE 3-14

Streaming video from the web on an iOS device

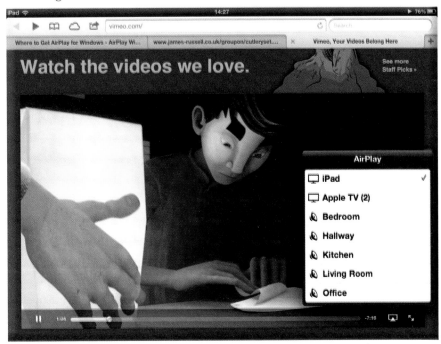

For apps that don't have an AirPlay button, try using the AirPlay button ( ) in the iOS multitasking dock (double-press the Home button, then scroll to the left until you see the AirPlay button) to stream to the Apple TV. This works, for example, with the TBS and CW video apps, which have no AirPlay button of their own.

If that doesn't work, you can try the screen-mirroring feature available in all iPads but the original model, the fifth-generation (late-2012 model) iPod Touch, and the iPhone 4S and later. But note that some apps, such as the NBC app, circumvent mirroring, so you can't watch their videos this way via an Apple TV either.

Here's how to mirror the iOS device's screen:

1. Make sure your Apple TV and iOS device are switched on and connected to the same network.

FIGURE 3-15

Streaming video from the NFL GamePass app to an Apple TV

2. Double-tap the Home button on your iOS device to open the multitasking dock at the bottom of the screen.

3. Swipe left across the row of icons in the dock until you see the AirPlay button (⟀).

4. Tap the AirPlay button (⟀) and select your Apple TV from the menu that appears.

5. Set the Mirroring switch to On. Your iOS device's screen will now appear on the TV connected to your Apple TV.

Stream only audio in video streaming from an iOS device

In some situations, you may want to stream only audio to an AirPlay device and keep the video on your iPad screen. For example, you might be watching a concert and want the audio to play through an AirPlay speaker or, as I often do, follow a recipe video on an iPad in your kitchen while the audio plays through the room's AirPlay speaker at a higher volume to drown out the sizzling.

This split-streaming is perfectly possible with any app that offers AirPlay streaming: Just select a speaker, not an Apple TV, from the list of available AirPlay devices so only the audio will stream over AirPlay, keeping the picture on your device's screen.

Stream video via AirPlay from a computer

As I've mentioned, Apple limits AirPlay video streaming on a computer to iTunes — just use the AirPlay button (◨) to the right of the playback controls to select your Apple TV — and to screen mirroring in OS X Mountain Lion if you have a compatible Mac (typically, a 2011 or later model). You can tell if your Mac supports screen mirroring because its icon in the menu bar is the AirPlay icon (◨) rather than the Displays icon (▤). Be sure your Apple TV is connected to the network; otherwise even your mirroring-compatible Mac will show the Displays icon (▤) instead of the AirPlay icon (◨) in the menu bar.

Here's how to mirror a screen from your Mac:

1. From the menu bar, choose ◨ ⇨ Apple TV (if you have more than one Apple TV, choose the one you want to mirror the display to).

That's it!

If you don't see the Apple TV option in the ◨ menu, go to the Displays system preference (choose ⇨ System Preferences, then click Displays) and check the Show Mirroring Options in the Menu Bar When Available option. While you're at it, choose Apple TV from the AirPlay mirroring pop-up menu in the Displays system preference, wait for the screen to refresh, and then make sure the Overscan Correction option is checked to optimize how the

Mac's screen fits on your TV screen. Then change the AirPlay mirroring option back to Off to resume normal Mac screen display (otherwise, your current screen stays mirrored to the Apple TV).

Slingbox and Other Streaming Alternatives

An Apple TV is the center of AirPlay video streaming, but there are additional purchases you can make to extend your viewing. For example, Slingbox sells a small box called the Slingbox that, when used with the $30 SlingPlayer software on your iOS device, lets you stream TV from your cable or satellite provider to your iOS device. (By itself, a Slingbox and its subscription service lets you watch your TV over the Internet from other locations, such as a hotel room while you are traveling.)

The Slingbox software also allows you to control playback on your box from your iOS device so you can switch channels, record content, and play content.

Elgato offers a similar product called EyeTV (yeah, it gets confusing when you throw the Apple TV into the mix) as well as options for satellite viewing and streaming over the web.

In both cases, the main benefits are obvious: You can watch your home TV service from anywhere you get an Internet connection, whether while on vacation, at a friend's house, or in the office (if you have a lenient boss). Although these products are a great option by themselves, they can add more capabilities to your AirPlay network, too. By using a device like the Slingbox or EyeTV, you can effectively stream content from a TV in one room to your mobile device and then to another TV via AirPlay, negating the need for another cable or satellite box in another room in your home. You can even watch your TV at other people's homes if they have an Apple TV in their living room. The quality won't quite match the original broadcast but, as technology advances and Internet speed becomes quicker, it's not far off.

A Day in the Life:
Streaming Music and Movies

It's a Sunday and you're checking e-mails at your computer. In your inbox, you find an announcement for a new album from your favorite band. You duly download it to iTunes and begin listening while you complete your weekend correspondence.

Before heading to the kitchen to wash up, you click the AirPlay button () in iTunes and select your AirPlay speaker in the kitchen so your music continues to play in another room.

The album features a bonus video track that you notice when accessing the album on your iPhone. The video is a little too epic for the small screen, so you head to the living room, play the video on your iPhone, and then use AirPlay to stream it to your Apple TV and watch it from the comfort of your sofa.

Friends come over for lunch so, while you're entertaining, you use iTunes on your computer to play your new album and you use Airfoil to send the audio stream to speakers dotted around your home.

A friend has a home movie from your school days stored on her iPad, so you give her access to your Wi-Fi network while everyone gathers around the TV. She sends the video via AirPlay to your Apple TV, controlling playback from her iPad.

You'll have to weigh the pros and cons of a box like this and also factor in the cost of the mobile app (for Slingbox at least) to see if it is an effective solution for you. I've used both and, if I left my desk more often, I could see real benefit to streaming TV content over the web to my iPhone or iPad.

While I'm on the subject of external devices, Elgato also sells its EyeTV tuners for iOS devices that allow you to receive free over-the-air television channels. Using a device like the EyeTV Mobile or EyeTV Micro with an iPhone or iPad could help you to access content that could be then streamed over AirPlay to your TV. If you're happy with the content you get from one of these little devices, you could almost forgo your cable subscription altogether.

If you're about to buy a new TV, check to see if it includes wireless or Ethernet connectivity as well as so-called "smart" features to help you bring together different media in one place without buying additional hardware. More and more connected TVs are capable of being controlled from an iOS device using apps like Zeebox that acts as a kind of digital assistant and is compatible with digital video recorder boxes too.

Aside from the Apple TV, you should investigate the Roku streaming media boxes that offer connections to favorite streaming platforms such as Netflix, Hulu, and Pandora. Like the Apple TV, they connect to your existing wireless network to pull media from your iTunes library. Another option is the Boxee box, which works in much the same way as the Roku box and Apple TV, connecting to your television and your wireless network to bring content from the web as well as your computer to your living room. You also can connect external drives to the Boxee box and send video to it directly from your iPad.

The Bluetooth Alternative to AirPlay

You can use Bluetooth for streaming audio to car stereos, portable speakers, and more from computers and iOS devices. Bluetooth also allows you to wirelessly control phones, remote control devices, wireless headsets, and other devices. Bluetooth is known for using a lot of power, but the Bluetooth Version 4 used in recent iOS devices, Macs, and other gadgets is much more power-efficient, so it won't drain your batteries too quickly. Apple's iOS software also does a great job managing Bluetooth power, so you can leave Bluetooth enabled in your iOS device (via the Settings app) without fear of draining your battery.

As an alternative to AirPlay, Bluetooth is reliable and effortless to use and doesn't require a Wi-Fi network, so you can use connected devices wherever you may be. Once a Bluetooth accessory has been paired with your computer or iOS device, its connection remains until you go out of range or turn off either device. Paired devices reconnect when they come within range of each other (and are turned on). Thus, Bluetooth makes it easier to access devices versus selecting them manually in AirPlay.

NOTE: Many Bluetooth devices can be connected to just one computer or iOS device at a time, requiring you pair and unpair to change your audio source. However, an increasing number of Bluetooth devices, such as car stereos, can be paired to at least two audio sources simultaneously.

Pair Bluetooth devices

To pair an iOS device to a Bluetooth device:

1. Launch the Settings app.
2. Tap the Bluetooth label to open the Bluetooth pane.
3. Set the Bluetooth switch to On.
4. Make your Bluetooth device is turned on. Some devices have a button or other control to enter pairing mode (see the user manual); put the Bluetooth device in pairing mode.
5. In a few seconds, the Bluetooth device should appear in the list of devices in the Settings app's Bluetooth pane. Tap the device's name to connect to it, as shown in Figure 3-16.
6. The device may automatically connect. Otherwise, the Settings app may ask you to enter a passcode or to confirm a passcode also shown on the device or noted in its manual. Consult the device's manual for how it pairs.

Compared to AirPlay-enabled speakers, the Bluetooth variety is far less expensive. Bluetooth speakers are often battery-powered, so you can charge them and take them

FIGURE 3-16

Pairing a Bluetooth device with an iPad

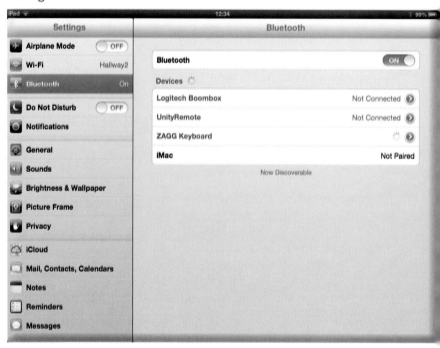

wherever you need without worrying about a power socket. When a Bluetooth speaker is turned on, you access it the same way you would an AirPlay speaker: from the AirPlay button (▲), as Figure 3-17 shows.

To pair a Mac to a Bluetooth device:

1. Launch System Preferences (choose ➪ System Preferences or click the System Preferences icon in the Dock).
2. Go to the Bluetooth system preference.
3. Check the boxes next to On and Discoverable.
4. Make your Bluetooth device is turned on. Some devices have a button or other control to enter pairing mode (see the user manual); put the Bluetooth device in pairing mode.
5. Click the Add button (the + icon) at the bottom of the Bluetooth system preference. In a few seconds, the

FIGURE 3-17

Streaming to a Bluetooth speaker via the AirPlay button ()

Bluetooth device should appear in the list of Bluetooth devices.

6. Select your speaker in the Bluetooth Setup Assistant dialog box that appears (see Figure 3-18) and click Continue.

7. The device may automatically connect. Otherwise, the Bluetooth Setup Assistant will ask you to enter a passcode or to confirm a passcode also shown on the device or noted in its manual. Consult the device's manual for how it pairs.

8. Click Quit.

If you connected an audio device, it should automatically be your default audio output device. If not, go to the Sound system preference's Output pane and click the Bluetooth device's name in the list to make it the active audio output. If the Bluetooth device still doesn't play your audio, go back to the Bluetooth system preference, select that Bluetooth

FIGURE 3-18

The Bluetooth Setup Assistant on a Mac

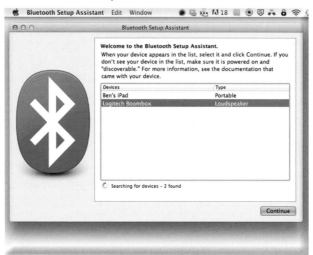

audio device, then choose the ⚙ ⇨ Use as Audio Device in the menu at the bottom of the Bluetooth system preference, or choose Use an Audio Device in the submenu for the Bluetooth device in the menu bar's Bluetooth menu (✳).

To pair a Windows PC to a Bluetooth device:

1. Go to the Control Panel (via the Start menu in Windows XP, Vista, and 7; via the Settings charm or the File Explorer in Windows 8).
2. In the Hardware and Sound section, click Add a Device.
3. Make sure your Bluetooth device is turned on. Some devices have a button or other control to enter pairing mode (see the user manual); put the Bluetooth device in pairing mode.
4. When your device appears in the Select a Device window, click it and then click the Next button to access the Setup Wizard.
5. Follow the instructions in the Setup Wizard to complete the installation.
6. Go to the Sound control panel to set the Bluetooth device as the PC's speaker.

Use Bluetooth speakers in an AirPlay network

How you use Bluetooth speakers in an AirPlay environment varies based on whether you are streaming music from an iOS device or a computer. Either way, you can't stream to both a Bluetooth and an AirPlay speaker at the same time.

In iOS, you select the Bluetooth speakers via the AirPlay menu, just as you would an AirPlay speaker. In OS X and Windows, you need to set your audio output to the Bluetooth device using the Sound system preference or Sound control panel, respectively — you can't use the AirPlay button () in iTunes to switch to a Bluetooth audio device).

If you've set your computer to use a Bluetooth speaker for audio output, you can switch to that speaker for audio output from the Music app on an iOS device using Apple's Remote app to select that computer as your output device, as described earlier in this chapter. You can also use a remote-access app such as iTeleport (see Chapter 9) to control what's playing on your computer.

4

Entertain Yourself from the Couch

AS WELL AS DISPLAY PHOTOS AND MUSIC, AIRPLAY CAN ENHANCE how you use your iOS devices for entertainment, such as for movies, TV shows, and games. An Apple TV is essential if you want the ultimate performance from your AirPlay network. If you haven't bought one yet, you can pick up one for about $100.

The latest model, released in early 2012, allows full HD streaming and includes enhanced Wi-Fi. There have been three iterations of Apple TV: The first one looked like a flattened Mac Mini, whereas the second and third looked more like ice hockey pucks. You want a puck, because the first-generation model doesn't provide the same level of connectivity and control as the newer devices. There's little reason to bother with the second-generation model, either, unless you get a big price break, because the third-generation model costs the same and provides better Wi-Fi performance and supports 1080p HD video (versus 720p HD for the second-generation model).

With an Apple TV connected to your network, you can boost how you use your TV. For a start, you can use your iPhone, iPad, or iPod Touch to play games on the big screen, using your device as a controller. Mirroring from an iOS device also makes a difference in how you watch sports. (In Chapter 9, I describe several amazing apps that improve your viewing options.)

You can use AirPlay to send video from apps that support AirPlay from any iPad, from an iPhone 4 or later model, or from a late-2010 or later model of the iPod Touch, as Chapter 3 explains. To mirror the device's screen via AirPlay, you need an iPhone 4S or later, fifth-generation (late 2012) model of the iPod Touch, or any iPad but the first model.

If it's running OS X Mountain Lion, you can even mirror the display of a recent-model (2011 or later), so you can send the display from your Mac to your HDTV via an Apple TV for an easy way to make presentations, watch Internet videos, and so on, as Chapter 3 explains.

More traditional features in the Apple TV include accessing media on your computer via iTunes and playing it on your TV via an Apple TV. This saves you having to move between rooms to set videos playing or rent movies and TV shows.

If you don't have an Apple TV, you can send video to a TV via physical cables. Apple sells cables that have an adapter to connect to an HDTV or other presentation device via an HDMI cable. It also sells cables that connect to a TV or other presentation device via a VGA cable; you'll need to connect the audio separately from the device's audio jack to an audio input on the TV. Likewise, there are similar adapters for the Mac. Prices range from $30 to $60.

Such physical connections are great for making presentations on the road when you can't be sure there's an Apple TV available, but at home they're inconvenient, as you have to have your devices close to your TV — that can work for playing movies but not so well when playing games. With the cost of an Apple TV so low, it just makes sense to make it your streaming center.

Play Games

With an iOS device and an Apple TV, games consoles can be a thing of the past, thanks to the wide range of games that use the mirroring feature. Some games simply show on your TV the iOS device's screen as is — so you play the game on your device and others can watch on the TV. Other games use the iOS device's screen as a secondary display. For example, Real Racing shows the main action on the TV screen, while your iOS device shows you just information such as the maps for the track you are racing on. Either way, you use the iOS device itself to play the game, such as maneuvering on the touchscreen and taking advantage of its accelerometer to tilt the device to steer a virtual car.

How games use Apple TV connectivity differs from app to app, but generally speaking you need to look for the AirPlay button () in the app to switch the display to the Apple TV. If the app has no AirPlay button, use the AirPlay controls in the multitasking dock in iOS to mirror the screen. For most games, expect to use the screen-mirroring capability in your iOS device, not a separate AirPlay control in the game itself.

Mirror games to an Apple TV

Most games that harness the Apple TV mirroring feature use the following technique to connect to a TV; however, you may need to adjust some settings specific to the app to work properly.

1. Launch the game you want to mirror to your Apple TV on your iOS device.
2. Double-press the Home button on your device.
3. Swipe from left to right across the row of icons that appears until you see the AirPlay button ().

FIGURE 4-1

Mirroring from an iOS device to an Apple TV with AirPlay

4. Tap the AirPlay button (◢) and choose your Apple TV from the menu that appears.

5. Set the Mirroring switch to On (see Figure 4-1). Your device's screen should appear on the TV.

6. Return to your app, so its screen appears on the TV. Some games will show the same thing on both screens, and some game will show controls on the iOS screen (as if it were a gaming console) and the main action on the TV screen.

Play multiplayer games

Some games, such as Scrabble and Trivial Pursuit, allow you to use multiple iOS devices with a single main display. In these games, an iPad takes the place of the traditional board, and each player's iPhone or iPod Touch becomes a tile rack or card, connected via Bluetooth or Wi-Fi to the iPad. Real Racing 2, for example, offers multiplayer gaming using as many as three iOS devices on a single Apple TV screen. You should search the App Store to find multiplayer games for your device; I note some my favorites in the next section of this chapter.

Games can use Bluetooth and/or Wi-Fi to connect to each other, so it's important that all your devices are connected to the same Wi-Fi network and have Bluetooth turned on. Use the following steps to set up Wi-Fi and Bluetooth on your iOS device and then head to the multiplayer section of your app to discover how to complete the setup.

1. Launch the Settings app.

2. Tap Wi-Fi and select the Wi-Fi network you want to use, then enter the password if requested.

3. Tap the Settings button at the top of the screen to return to the main Settings menu.

4. Tap Bluetooth.

5. Set the Bluetooth switch to On.

Play multiplayer games online

Many of the games in the App Store allow you to compete online against other players. Apps like Words with Friends and Letterpress let you take a turn and be notified when your opponents take theirs, while games like Air Wings and N.O.V.A let you show off your skills in real time in the same way as a console game.

If you're keen to try out some of the best multiplayer games for iOS as well as use games that offer mirroring features for the Apple TV, you can't get much better than these gems:

- A favorite in my house is Electronic Arts' Scrabble, the traditional board game redesigned for iOS that lets you use your iPhone or iPod Touch as tile holder while an iPad becomes the main board.
- For sports lovers, EA Sports' FIFA series offers local multiplayer features so you can take on your friends in soccer matches using a Wi-Fi connection and two devices — and even use AirPlay mirroring to an Apple TV.
- Of course, you can't beat Real Racing 2 if you want to the mirroring options from an iOS game.
- If you like its console games, Modern Combat 3 is another AirPlay mirroring-enabled shooter you'll enjoy.
- For a more arcade feel, I definitely recommend Chopper 2, which also includes mirroring so you can play on your TV using your iOS device to control the on screen action.

How you find and connect to your adversaries differs depending on the app, with some using their own servers, others using Facebook and Twitter, and still others using Apple's Game Center, which I describe next. Almost all these apps require having an account with the game provider; in some cases, the e-mail address you provide lets friends discover that you are playing the same game, either by searching for your e-mail address or the game checking your contacts list to see what players match entries there.

FIGURE 4-2

The Game Center app

Play with others via Game Center

For a quick and easy way to find friends to play games against, view your achievements, and discover new games, your best bet is Game Center (see Figure 4-2), Apple's gaming hub. Game Center is available on iOS devices and Macs, and you can sign in using your Apple ID.

Friends who are using Game Center are listed in the app, so you can challenge them to a head-to-head game whenever you fancy from your chosen app. They'll see you in their Game Center app as well. How? Game Center taps into your contacts list and compares e-mail addresses in everyone's list to those people provided to the Game Center app to see who knows who. So, the more e-mail addresses to your Game Center account, the more likely friends will see you in their Game Centers.

If your friends aren't hard-core gamers, you can use Game Center's Auto Match feature to find opponents you don't know who are also looking for a game.

Only apps compatible with Apple's social gaming network work with Game Center; there's a handy Find Game Center Games in the Game Center app that lists Game Center-ready titles in the App Store. All your games compatible with Game Center are also listed in the Game Center app.

Game Center also provides leaderboard information for games, so you can see how you match up with the rest of the world.

If you use the same game on both an iOS device and your Mac, many games will allow you to access the same Game Center account so you can play multiplayer games and set high scores on any of your devices.

To use Game Center, you first need to be signed in to the Game Center app on all your devices. That's all some games

FIGURE 4-3

Sending an invite with Game Center

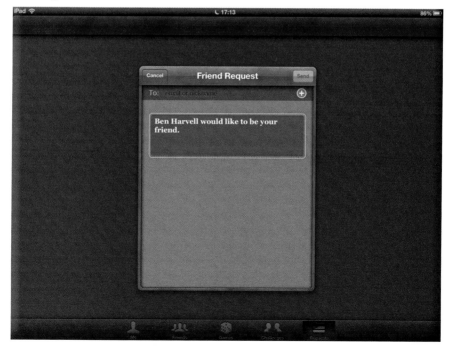

need, but others will require you sign in to them when you launch the app.

Then you want to invite friends to play with you. Here's how:

1. Launch the Game Center app from your iOS device or Mac.
2. Enter your Apple ID and password to login.
3. Tap the Friends button at the bottom of the window to view your friends and recommendations.
4. Tap the Requests button at the bottom of the window.
5. Tap the Add Friends button or the Add button (the + icon) at the top of the window.
6. Enter the e-mail address of the person you want to add as a friend.
7. Type a message in the field below or leave it as it is.
8. Tap the Send button to send your friend request (see Figure 4-3).

Use gaming subscription services and stores

For many years, the Mac wasn't seen as a viable gaming platform, but it recently has come into its own, with major titles available for download from the Mac App Store as well as other stores like Steam (see Figure 4-4).

Steam (http://store.steampowered.com) served only PC gamers for years, but now offers some of the best games available for Mac, as well as a convenient way to store them that works the same way as the Mac App Store. You can download games on multiple computers once you've purchased them from Steam, and all updates are delivered through the Steam client as well. You can also use Steam to set up multiplayer games or chat with other users while playing.

Another gaming service, OnLive (www.onlive.com), takes gaming across even more of your devices: It supports Macs, PCs, and iOS devices, and it streams (yes, streams)

FIGURE 4-4

The Steam service on a Mac

games directly to your device from its mammoth Internet servers. OnLive brings a new dimension to online gaming because users aren't restricted by the platforms they are on, so Mac and iPad users can play games that were designed for Windows, for example. Internet-based gaming also means that you can pick up where you left off in a game on whatever device you choose, as long as it's connected to the OnLive system. Subscribers to OnLive can access any game on the system for a monthly fee and play for as long as they like without additional costs.

Accessorize your gaming

As evidenced by the numerous iPhone and iPad cases, battery packs, and more on the market, manufacturers know they're on to a good thing. That same business opportunity exists on the gaming side of iOS, so you can take your iOS gaming experience to the next level with accessories that turn your device into a hard-core entertainment machine.

For example, the original and still brilliant Ion iCade Arcade Cabinet for iPad (www.ionaudio.com) converts your tablet into a retro arcade machine complete with joystick and buttons. There's even a coin slot (although you don't actually have to spend money each time you play like you used to). Compatible with a vast selection of iOS games, the iCade connects via Bluetooth. It costs $130, but is often sold for $60 to $100.

Cheaper at $80 (but often sold for around $40) is the Duo Gamer (www.duo-games.com), an Apple-approved game controller for iOS devices. Although the controller is fairly ugly, it offers a selection of controls akin to a modern console and is compatible with all Gameloft's current iOS titles. Annoyingly, that's as far as this device goes, lacking support for any other iOS games.

At the cheaper end of the spectrum are the $10 ThinkGeek Joystick-It Arcade Stick for iPad (www.thinkgeek.com) and the $30 ThinkGeek iCade 8-Bitty, two lightweight controllers for iOS devices with very different approaches. The Joystick-It is ingenious in that it sticks to the screen of an iPad with a suction cup, providing you with a joystick to control any iOS game that uses a virtual control pad. The iCade 8-Bitty is a Nintendo-esque controller that connects to iOS devices via Bluetooth and provides a simple way to control games without getting the screen too grubby with constant taps and swipes. With buttons as well as a control pad, the iCade 8-Bitty offers a little more control than a virtual control.

Remote-Control Your Entertainment

With an iOS device by your side, you have a unique and endlessly useful remote control at hand. Whether you want to control your Apple TV, your Mac, or even your video recorder

FIGURE 4-5

The Remote app lists available Apple TVs and iTunes libraries so you can remote-control them.

in some cases, an iOS device can do it all without you leaving the sofa. Getting up to look for a specific remote or find a movie or any other file on your computer will be a thing of the past. For this couch-potato nirvana to become real, all your devices need to be connected to the same Wi-Fi network and be switched on.

Control an Apple TV from an iOS device

Apple's free Remote app lets you use an iOS device as a remote control for your Apple TV, allowing you to browse, search, and stream more easily. Unlike the physical remote that comes with your Apple TV, the Remote app allows you to use gestures on your iOS device to control the onscreen menus. That's a lot easier than clicking left, right, up, or down. The app is also a godsend for searching with keywords, allowing you to use the iOS onscreen keyboard to type rather than enter individual

The Remote app controlling an Apple TV

letters using the physical remote to move through a list of letters and select each one in turn.

Once your iOS device is connected to the same Wi-Fi network as your Apple TV, follow these steps to control your Apple TV with the Remote app.

1. Launch the Remote app.
2. If an icon for the Apple TV doesn't appear on screen, tap the Device Select button.
3. Tap the Apple TV you want to use from the list of Apple TVs and iTunes libraries (see Figure 4-5).

Now you can use the Remote app as a remote. Tap the Control button (✛) at the bottom of the Remote screen on an iPhone or iPod Touch; it's at the upper right of the screen on an iPad. You now have several controls:

▶ Drag your finger up, down, left, or right in the navigation area that appears in the middle of the screen (see Figure 4-6) to move between sections on the Apple TV screen. Dragging to the left, for example, performs the same action as clicking the left button on the physical remote.

▶ While a video or song is playing, slide a finger to the left or right to fast-forward or rewind, respectively. The

FIGURE 4-7

Searching on the Remote app

farther you drag your finger, the faster the media will skip.

○ Tap a finger to select an item; doing so performs the same action as clicking the Select button on the physical remote.

○ Tap Menu to go back to the previous item or option.

○ Tap Play/Pause (▶ǀǀ) to toggle between playing and pausing the current audio or video.

○ Tap the Contextual Menu button (▤) to pull up extra features for the current item, if available. (The physical remote has no equivalent to this button). For example, when playing a menu, tapping this button brings up a list of chapters so you can jump to the one you want. When listing podcasts, pressing the button displays the Mark as Played option on the TV screen, which you can then "click" by tapping the Remote app's screen.

Rather than selecting one letter at a time with the Apple TV remote to do a search, such as for a movie title, you can use the Remote app and type searches using the iOS device's onscreen keyboard. You can also the iOS onscreen keyboard to enter e-mail addresses and passwords, such as when

THE MIRACLE OF MUSIC RECOGNITION

If you're not familiar with apps like Shazam or SoundHound, you're really missing a trick. It's more than likely that you've heard a song on the radio, on TV, or even in a bar and thought, "I wonder who this is?" at one point in your life. Unless you're lucky enough to have friends with encyclopedic music knowledge nearby or you're the sort of person who pesters DJs, a number of great tunes will have passed you by.

That's what Shazam (shown at left) and SoundHound address. With them, you use your iOS device to find the name of the track playing, the name of the artist, the album it came from and, most important, where you can buy it. Basically, you have them listen to the music through your iOS device's microphone, then they match it from their exhaustive database.

But they can do more than just identify the song and tell you where to buy it. Shazam, for example, allows you to view on YouTube the video for the song you've "tagged," check out when the band or artist is touring, share who you're listening to on Twitter, and even see the lyrics for the song currently playing.

SoundHound offers similar features, plus has the unique trick of allowing you to sing or hum into it and, in most situations, determine the song (if your singing or humming is relatively accurate).

Believe it or not, I have it on good authority that musicians use such apps when composing new songs to make sure they're not ripping off another artist's work.

signing in to Home Sharing or your iTunes account, using the Remote app:

1. Navigate to the search interface on your Apple TV, such as the iTunes Movies search.
2. Drag your finger across the Remote app's screen until the search field is highlighted. The onscreen keyboard will appear on the iOS device. iPhones and iPod Touches also vibrate at this point.
3. Type your search words using the iOS onscreen keyboard (see Figure 4-7). Your search results will appear on your TV's screen.
4. Tap the Hide button to close the iOS onscreen keyboard.

Access your iTunes content through an Apple TV

With your Apple TV connected to the same network as your computer, you can play all the content in your iTunes library on your TV: Browse movies, music, and TV shows in your living room without touching your computer.

To access your iTunes content on your Apple TV, you need to turn on Home Sharing. Once enabled, it stays that way until you change it, so this is a set-once-and-forget activity. Ensure that Apple TV is connected to the same network as your computer via Wi-Fi or Ethernet, then follow these steps:

1. Go to the Settings section on your Apple TV's Home screen.
2. Select Computers.
3. Select Turn On Home Sharing.
4. Enter your Home Sharing username and password. This is normally your Apple ID, but some people use a separate ID; either way, it needs to be the same username and password as set up for Home Sharing in iTunes on your computer.
5. If Home Sharing is not already enabled on your computer, go to iTunes on your computer, choose File

⇨ Home Sharing ⇨ Turn on Home Sharing. You can set up Home Sharing on multiple computers so they are all available to the Apple TV, but only those using the same Home Sharing username and password as the Apple TV are shown.

Once Home Sharing is enabled on the Apple TV and your computers, you'll see all available iTunes libraries in the Computers section of the Apple TV screen, as well as in the Remote app. Make sure iTunes is running on the computers whose iTunes libraries you want to play through the Apple TV to your TV — otherwise, those libraries aren't available even if the computers are turned on.

Play content from your iTunes library from your Apple TV

Once your Apple TV is connected to your iTunes library, all the stored music, movies, TV shows, and podcasts can be played on your TV:

1. From your Apple TV's Home screen, select Computers.
2. Select the iTunes library you want to access, if there's more than one available.
3. Select from the list of available content such as Music, Movies, TV Shows, and Podcasts.
4. Select the media you want to play.

TIP: When playing music or podcasts via your Apple TV to your stereo system, you need the TV on to see what you're selecting, whether from the Remote app or the physical remote that comes with the Apple TV. But once your music or podcast is playing through the stereo, you can turn off the TV. That will also cause the Apple TV to stop playing. However, all you need to do is press the Play/Pause button (▶ǁ) to have the audio resume, even though the TV screen is off. Of course, if you're using the TV's speakers to play the audio, you need to leave the TV turned on.

Use the iTunes Store on an Apple TV

As well as accessing content on your computer via an Apple TV, you can purchase and rent movies and TV shows in both high definition (HD) and standard definition from the iTunes Store right from your TV — no computer required. You can even add items to a wish list so you can quickly find them in the future. Alternatively, for TV shows, you can purchase a season pass that provides the latest episode of a particular show when it has aired on broadcast or cable TV.

Each video on the Apple TV includes a preview as well as additional information such as reviews from Rotten Tomatoes and from iTunes customers.

TIP: The Apple TV lets you get content from more than the iTunes Store and your computer's iTunes library. It also supports YouTube, Vimeo, Flickr, Internet-based "radio stations," several sports networks, and — if you're a subscriber — Netflix and Hulu Plus. You'll see buttons on the Apple TV's Home screen for all these content sources.

Change the default video resolution on an Apple TV

The second-generation (late 2010) Apple TV model by default shows 720p HD content to rent or buy via the Apple TV but you can change this setting to access SD (standard definition) content, which downloads faster and usually looks just fine on smaller TVs. The third-generation (early 2012) Apple TV model by default shows 1080p HD content, which you can change to either 720p HD or SD, both of which take less time to download at the price of reduced resolution. (The first-generation Apple TV only shows SD video.) There's also no reason to download HD versions of movies and TV shows if you're not watching them on an HDTV. To change the default quality setting:

WATCH CABLE AND SATELLITE TV ON YOUR iOS DEVICE

A number of major cable providers offer apps for mobile viewing on your iOS device, not just apps to remote-control their set-top boxes. Bear in mind, however, that most of these services restrict your viewing to your home network through a router provided by your cable provider.

COMCAST: The Xfinity TV Player app for iOS devices allows Comcast subscribers to access their existing channels over Wi-Fi, control their TV, and schedule remote recordings.

TIME WARNER CABLE: The TWC TV app offers control over your set-top box and parental controls , plus — if you're connected to your home Wi-Fi network — the ability to watch shows and sports on your iPad, iPhone, or iPod Touch.

COX COMMUNICATIONS: Cox TV Connect allows you to watch TV on your iPad if you are using your home's Wi-Fi connection. Cox also has a version for iPhones and iPod Touches.

CABLEVISION: The Optimum for iPad app offers all the channels you get through your Cablevision subscription and also controls your DVR and schedule recordings. But it works only on your home Wi-Fi network if you also have the Optimum cable modem. There's also a version for iPhones and iPod Touches.

BRIGHT HOUSE NETWORKS: Same deal here: Any channels you get via your DVR are available on your iOS device only through the Bright House TV app if you're connected to your home Wi-Fi network.

WATCHESPN: For subscribers to ESPN via Time Warner Cable, Bright House Networks, or Verizon FiOS, the WatchESPN app is your route to mobile sports viewing on your iOS device. The app is free and you simply need a username and password from your provider to access as many of the ESPN channels available via your cable or satellite provider. And you aren't restricted to watching from your home network.

SKY GO: For users of the U.K.'s BSkyB satellite TV service, the Sky Go app offers a selection of channels, including sports, movies, and news. The app is free to subscribers and works on iOS devices over Wi-Fi and cellular connections — again, you're not limited to watching from your home's Wi-Fi network.

1. Navigate to the Settings button on the Apple TV's Home screen and select it.
2. Select iTunes Store in the list that appears.
3. Select Video Resolution in the list that appears; each time you select this option, the Apple TV cycles to the next available option: 1080p HD, 720p HD, and SD on a third-generation Apple TV and 720p HD and SD on a second-generation Apple TV.

Rent or buy movies and TV shows on an Apple TV

Renting is an easy way to watch a movie without buying it and taking up the space on your computer to save it. It's like renting a movie from your local video store but with far less effort. Rentals are charged to your iTunes Store account and must be viewed within 30 days of renting. Once you start the movie, you have 24 hours to finish watching it. You can also buy movies, which differs from renting them in that you can watch them as many times as you want forever.

1. From the Apple TV's Home screen, navigate to the Movies icon and select it.
2. Scroll to view new and popular movies as well as movies organized by category, or use the links at the top of the screen to view genres, find recommended movies based on your taste with Apple's Genius feature, or to search for a specific film.
3. When you have selected the film you want to rent, the details screen appears. Scroll across to the Rent button, which shows whether the rental is in HD or standard definition and how much the rental costs. Click the button to rent the movie. Or select the Buy button to buy the movie.
4. You are asked to confirm the rental or purchase by clicking OK, after which you can begin watching your movie.

TV GUIDE APPS

Getting the *TV Guide* as a magazine or skipping through channels on your set-top box isn't the most efficient way to find something to watch on TV. No, what you need is to reach out and touch the listings — tap to read descriptions of each show and set your channel listing so you see only your favorite channels without the more obscure broadcasts getting in the way. Well, lucky for you, there are a bunch of apps that let you do just that on your iOS devices.

Being a Brit, I use the TVGuide.co.uk app (shown below) on my iPad. Its TV Guide app allows users to remotely record shows if they have a compatible digital video recorder.

For those of you across the pond, there's the TV Guide Mobile app from the folks at TVGuide.com available. It offers some incredibly social features, including a list of the trending shows and the ability to share what you're watching with others directly from the app.

Both apps allow you to see what is showing on specific channels at certain times and allow you to customize the channels shown so you see only the content you're looking for. Compared to a physical TV guide, these apps — along with the many others available in the App Store — are far superior thanks to their customizable nature and more up-to-date listings.

The process for TV shows is similar, though you can only purchase them, not rent them. You can buy individual episodes by selecting them and then purchasing that episode, or you can select the Purchase Season Pass option at the top of the episode list to purchase that entire season.

Add movies and TV shows to your Apple TV's wish list

The Apple TV's wish list feature is a handy way to save the titles of films so you can quickly find them at a later date. Each movie available via the iTunes Store has a Wish List button in its details screen that, when selected, adds that video to your wish list. (Select it again to remove it from the wish list.) You access your wish list from the top of the Movies section of the Apple TV's Home screen; select a film from the list to begin the rental or purchase process. To remove a movie from your wish list, go back to its details screen and click the Remove button.

There's a similar option for TV shows called *favorites*. When viewing TV shows in the iTunes Store, select the Add to Favorites button to add them to your Favorites list, shown at the top of the TV Shows section of the Apple TV's Home screen. If a TV show is marked as a favorite, that button changes to Remove from Favorites; select it to remove it from the favorites list.

Get movie and TV recommendations from your Apple TV

The Genius feature in iTunes is also available via the Apple TV; it offers a convenient way to be introduced to new films and TV shows based on your previous purchases. On the Apple TV's Home screen, at the top of the Movies and TV Shows section is the Genius option. Select it to get recommendations for movies and TV shows that Genius considers similar to those you've bought or rented through the iTunes Store.

WATCH MORE SPORTS WITH YOUR iOS DEVICE

Here's one of the big draws of the iOS platform: watching live sports at home or elsewhere with just a few taps. Even better, not all these methods cost money. They could also help you avoid restrictions on certain games in your area, giving you access to more games than you would find from your local station. Where once you were limited by the choice of game from your chosen channels and location, you now have the option to access almost any game you want by signing up to the right package or accessing the right apps. A decent data plan or a Wi-Fi connection should be all you need once you have the correct apps on your device.

BASEBALL: The ultimate baseball app, if not the best sports app overall, MLB at Bat provides a unique way to follow the baseball season including live streaming (with an MLB.TV subscription), highlights, and audio commentary. Better yet, it provides live stats that can be placed over the video stream to show a multitude of information including box scores, player stats, and even where individual pitches were aimed.

The app's price changes each year but is typically about $15. It's also available directly from the Apple TV's Home screen.

In offseason periods, MLB.TV subscribers can to watch any game from the regular season. During the regular season, all games are streamed, with nonsubscribers able to purchase a single game stream at a time. An MLB.TV subscription costs around $100 for the premium package that will allow you to view all games in the MLB season.

FOOTBALL: NFL GamePass (see the figure at upper right) is my personal favorite service, with its online and app-based streaming of every game from the NFL season and additional packages for pre- and post-season games. You can quickly find the game you are after and watch it right on your iOS device or stream it to your TV via AirPlay. You also get access to NFL Network 24 hours a day and, in some territories (though not in the U.K.) NFL RedZone. A subscription is surprisingly cheap at $40, and it works over both Wi-Fi and

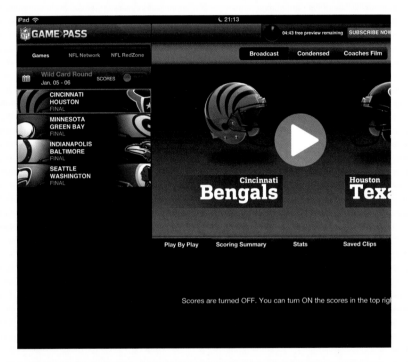

cellular networks. Note local games are blacked out.

Frustratingly, NFL Mobile is available only to Verizon Wireless

 customers, for whom it is a treat. On the iPad, you can use the Game Center feature that includes live audio and drive charts as well as scores and stats. On the iPhone, you can access NFL RedZone as well as NFL Network, ESPN Monday Night Football, NBC Sunday Night Football, and NFL Thursday Night Football, plus Game Center with in-game highlights.

BASKETBALL: How you watch live games from the NBA depends largely on your location. Users need to link their existing (U.S.) cable or satellite account (if supported) or purchase an NBA League Pass Broadband subscription for the web and mobile only for $99. From there, you choose the app specific to your location.

For example, a long time ago, I must have bought an episode of *Lost* on my Apple TV because now when I select the Genius option in the TV Shows section on my Apple TV, I am recommended shows such as *24* and *Prison Break*. Sure, the Apple TV isn't offering me particularly up-to-date choices, but then I probably watched that *Lost* episode about five years ago.

Likewise, I purchased the movie *The Hangover*, so Genius believes I would like to watch *Anchorman* and *American Pie*. As a matter of fact, I've seen both but then the Apple TV doesn't know that because it only knows what I've watched through the iTunes Store.

Control Set-Top Boxes and Other Devices

I've mentioned products like the Slingbox in Chapter 3 that allow you to view and control your home cable or satellite box remotely. There are also a few providers that offer apps that allow you to control your set-top box on a local network. DirecTV, Comcast, and AT&T in the U.S. all provide free apps for their customers that replace the traditional remote control in favor of an iOS device app. In the U.K., the Sky+ app offers the same control for Sky subscribers, as Figure 4-8 shows.

If you have a modern digital video recorder and a subscription with a major TV provider, it's worth checking to see if it provides an app, so you can rid your living room of unwanted remotes. If you use a media service such as a TiVo or Roku, there are also apps available in the App Store that allow you to control them from your iPhone, iPad, or iPod Touch.

For your home stereo and other entertainment gear, you can also use your iOS device as a remote control. Some network-connectible stereos receivers and Blu-ray players from Panasonic, LG, and others have free remote-control apps in the App Store that you can use to control them from your iOS device.

FIGURE 4-8

Controlling a Sky set-top box with the Sky+ app

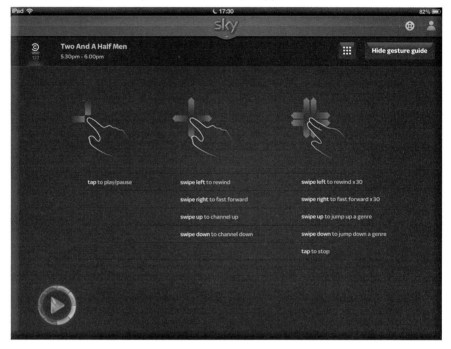

Then there's Gear4's $100 UnityRemote (www.gear4.com), a combo of an infrared (IR) blaster and iOS app that lets you control non-networked home theater equipment from your iOS device. Basically, the device connects to your iOS device over Wi-Fi, and then sends IR beams in all directions in hopes of reaching your home theater equipment. Traditional remotes send an IR beam to their devices, which is why you have to point the remotes accurately at them. If you can find a place in your living room where the UnityRemote's IR beams can reach all your devices, it's a great way to get rid of all those individual remotes — and lets you switch among all your devices from one screen. (Of course, should you not have your iOS device with you, you can always use the original remotes.)

The UnityRemote includes a database of common controls for a wide range of popular devices and brands. If your device isn't in the database, you can "teach" the IR blaster and app that device's control commands. For more on universal remote controls, see Chapter 9.

Some cable and satellite providers offer a "multi-room" add-on allowing users to have more than one set-top box in their home to watch different channels in different rooms — for an extra monthly fee that can add up over time.

A cheaper option is to send the signal from your main set-top box to that other TV in your bedroom, using what's called an *AV sender device*. The prices of these devices differ wildly, so you'll need to shop around to get a good deal. An AV sender with wireless connectivity and HD quality will be the most expensive option. The 5.8GHz AV senders also cost more, but they avoid interference with Wi-Fi networks and cordless phones that the 2.4GHz AV senders often experience.

Of course, AV senders make you walk back to your set-top box to do simple things like change the channel. You could use an IR blaster to extend the range of your remote control, but IR blasters need a direct line of sight, so unless your living room has a clear view of your bedroom, they won't help.

A better option is to use a remote device and app such as the UnityRemote mentioned previously. As long as your iOS device is in range of the UnityRemote's Bluetooth hub, you can control the "master" TV's set-top box in the other room. If your TV service provider offers an iOS remote-control app, you don't need something like UnityRemote, as long as the set-top box is connected to your home network and thus the Internet to receive commands from your remote-control app.

5

Take, Sync, and Share Photos

PHOTOGRAPHY, AIRPLAY, AND ICLOUD GO HAND IN HAND IF you're using an iOS device.

At its most basic level, Photo Stream allows you to take a photo on one device, (let's say your iPhone) and, assuming all is set up correctly, access that same photo a few seconds later on your computer, your iPad, iPod Touch, or Apple TV. Once you get used to Photo Stream, it's likely you'll wonder how you were able to live without it.

As a tech journalist, I use Photo Stream on a daily basis for adding screenshots of iOS devices to articles I write. No need for iOS simulators on the desktop, connecting my device to my computer to sync the screens, or sending screenshots by e-mail anymore. Once the shot is taken, it appears on my computer a few seconds later.

That's just one very niche use of the technology. For the everyday consumer, there are huge benefits. Photos of a day out snapped on your iPhone are ready and waiting to be gathered in an iPhoto gallery on your iPad or computer when you get home. Creatives sharing inspiration with others can quickly snap a photo or grab an image on their iPad's screen and send it to a shared Photo Stream for others to see. Business users can send images from their iOS device or laptop to an Apple TV as part of a presentation. The list goes on and on.

Beyond Photo Stream, there are many ways to share photos taken on your iPhone, iPad, or iPod Touch using built-in iOS features. Whether you want to fire photos to your friends via e-mail, upload images to social networking sites like Facebook and Twitter, or print them out, you can do so with a few taps on your iOS device's screen (see Figure 5-1) thanks to the Sharing pop-over supported in many apps.

And there's more! You can set your Apple TV to show your most recent photos, apply images to contacts, use photos as a screen saver, and giving great slideshows without spending hours with a projector and a box of negatives. Believe me, at least for the last tip, your friends and family will thank you for it.

FIGURE 5-1

Sharing photos from an iOS device is easier than ever, thanks to the Sharing pop-over.

Set Up Photo Stream

When you first set up your iPhone, iPod Touch, or iPad or added an iCloud account to any of these devices, you were probably asked if you wanted to set up Photo Stream as well. It doesn't really matter if you did; it's simple enough to check whether it's up and running: Head to your device's Settings app and tap the iCloud label. A list of iCloud features in the iCloud pane, showing which are enabled. It also shows the name of the iCloud account you are using on the device. If you see none of that, iCloud isn't set up on your device, so you'll need to head back to Chapter 1 and follow the instructions there to add or create an iCloud account.

If iCloud is running on your device, scroll to the Photo Stream section in the Settings app's iCloud pane, shown in Figure 5-2, and make sure that Photo Stream is switched on.

FIGURE 5-2

Check whether Photo Stream is turned on from the Settings app's iCloud pane.

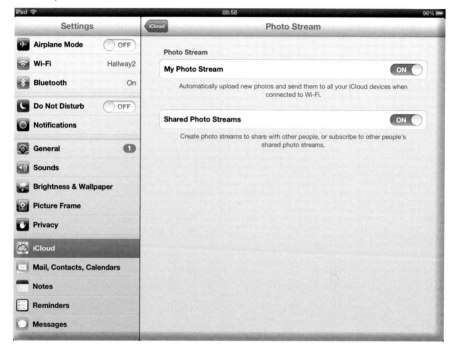

While you're at it, you may as well turn on Shared Photo Streams too unless you're sure you never want to use the feature (I explain it later in this chapter). Now is also a good time to make sure that you have the same iCloud account running on all the devices you want to share photos among, be they computers, iPhones, iPads, or iPod Touches.

You were probably expecting a little more detail on the Photo Stream setup process, I'm sure, but it's literally as easy as flicking a switch on an iOS device. But for computers, the process is a little different but ultimately comes down to the same switch. Mac users will likely have iCloud already running on their computer but, if not, head back to Chapter 1 and make sure it's set up. The same goes for Windows users using the iCloud control panel: If it's installed, great. If not, it's back to Chapter 1 for you.

FIGURE 5-3

Editing Photo Stream settings on a Mac

With iCloud set up on your computer, you need to make sure Photo Stream is switched on. Mac users can do this from the iCloud system preference (see Figure 5-3) while PC users need to switch it on via the iCloud control panel (which is usually available in the Network and Internet group).

On a Mac, the Photo Stream images appear in the iPhoto app that comes with new Macs, in the Photo Stream section. (You will need to buy a copy from the Mac App Store if you don't have it preinstalled.) Windows PC users' Photo Stream images are stored in their My Pictures folder by default, although you can set a different location for the photos via the iCloud control panel's Options button.

Once you have switched on Photo Stream on your iOS device, you'll notice that a new section is available in the Photos app. Unsurprisingly, it's called Photo Stream, and it includes any photos you have taken with your device in the last 30 days or since Photo Stream was turned on — whichever comes last.

These photos also appear on any of your other devices linked to the same iCloud account that also have Photo Stream turned on. You can think of this Photo Stream section as a shared gallery of all the pictures you have taken. As you take them, your device uploads them to Apple's iCloud server (if you have an Internet connection, of course) and then downloads them to your other Photo Stream-enabled devices (again, if they're connected to the Internet).

Photo Stream's syncing approach also means that deleting a picture from the Photo Stream on any device deletes the picture from all your other devices, too. So if you want to keep a copy of an image permanently, copy it to a folder on your Mac from iPhoto or copy it to a different folder on your PC — those copies out of Photo Stream's default locations are *not* deleted when you delete the image from a Photo Stream location.

SHARE VIDEO STREAMS

Although it would drain bandwidth, increase cellular data charges, and slow down your iOS device, it would still be pretty neat to have Photo Stream share videos to all your devices, not just the photos you shoot.

If you're desperate for that function, you can always get KendiTech's Video Stream for iCloud from the App Store. As the name suggests, the app syncs video clips among all your iOS devices and uses iCloud to do it.

TIP: Uploading and downloading photos over a cellular connection can eat up your data plan quickly. Which is why iOS devices don't do that — they only upload and download Photo Stream images when they have a Wi-Fi connection to the Internet. But if you use the Shared Photo Stream feature described later in this chapter, it *does* use cellular connections, and the only way to stop that is to turn off the feature in the iCloud pane of the Settings app: Tap Photo Streaming to see the settings.

Test your Photo Stream

Now that you've set up Photo Stream, it's worth giving it a quick test. Take a photo on one of your iOS devices and check that it appears in the Photo Stream section of the Photos app. Now wait a minute or so and check your other devices in turn to make sure the image has appeared in the Photo Stream there, too.

If the image doesn't appear on your other devices, first make sure they and the device you took the image on are connected to the Internet via Wi-Fi. If the Internet connection wasn't the issue, try turning Photo Stream off and on again (an oldie but a goodie) to renew the connection. If neither of these techniques work, make sure you are using the same iCloud account on all your devices.

Extra features for iPhoto users

As you might expect, Photo Stream is well supported on Macs, so there are a few settings in iPhoto that PC users don't have equivalents for in the iCloud control panel. In iPhoto, adjust these options in the Photo Stream pane in the Preferences dialog box (choose iPhoto ⇨ Preferences), shown in Figure 5-4. You can adjust several settings such as automatic imports and uploads, which are handy for keeping your Photo Stream organized by adding images that you import to iPhoto to the Photo Stream on all your devices. The Automatic Import feature allows you to add Photo Stream

FIGURE 5-4

iPhoto's Photo Stream settings

photos to other iPhoto collections such as Events, Photos, Faces, and Places so you don't create a separate selection of photos from your camera. Additionally, Shared Photo Streams also can get their own section in iPhoto.

Share Photo Streams

While your photos in Photo Stream are shared among all your connected devices, you use Shared Photo Streams (see Figure 5-5) to share photos with other people. A Shared Photo Stream is effectively a gallery of photos you select and is controlled from any of your iCloud-connected devices. Let's say, for example, that you go on holiday and want to share photos from your trip with friends and family back home. All you need to do is create a Shared Photo Stream and invite contacts to view it.

Whenever you want to share a photo, rather than attach it to an e-mail or share your entire Photo Stream, you simply send the image to the Shared Photo Stream you created and all those people you invited will be able to see it and, in some cases, be notified that a new photo has been added. This is a handy alternative to Facebook or Twitter and is more personal than uploading images to a social media site because you can quickly set who sees the photos and upload them without having to worry about adjusting privacy settings each time.

FIGURE 5-5

Shared Photo Streams

Friends can access your Shared Photo Stream on an iOS device, a Mac, or on the web, and they can even "like" photos and add comments if they want.

You can create and add photos to a Shared Photo Stream on an iPhone, iPad, or iPod Touch running iOS 6, from iPhoto 9.4 or later or Aperture 3.4 or later on a Mac running OS X Mountain Lion, and via Windows Explorer on PCs running Windows Vista or later and the iCloud control panel; invites are sent via e-mail.

To see a Shared Photo Stream, people need an iPhone, iPad, or iPod Touch running iOS 6 (the images are viewed in the Photos app) or a Mac running OS X Mountain Lion and iPhoto (where the images are viewed). Otherwise, they'll have to use a web browser to access the Shared Photo Stream via the link that is e-mailed to them when you share the stream.

Create a Shared Photo Stream on an iOS device

Creating a Shared Photo Stream on an iOS device is a simple process:

1. In the Photos app, select an album, your Photo Stream, or your entire photo library (the Camera Roll) to view the pictures.
2. Tap the Edit button.
3. Scroll through your photos and tap each one you want to add to your Shared Photo Stream. A check mark appears on each image you have selected (see Figure 5-6).
4. Tap the Share button (📤) and then tap Photo Stream from the pop-over that appears.
5. If you've already set up a Shared Photo Stream, you can now select it from the list. Or you can tap New Photo Stream to create a new one.

FIGURE 5-6

Selecting images to add to a Photo Stream

FIGURE 5-7

Sharing a Photo Stream with others

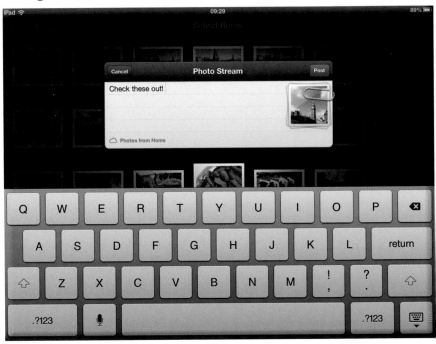

6. Enter the name or e-mail address of each person you want to share your Photo Stream with, name the Photo Stream, and set the Public Website setting to On or Off. If you set it to Off, only iCloud users you invite will be able to view your Shared Photo Stream.

7. Tap the Next button and optionally enter a comment for those you have shared the Photo Stream with (see Figure 5-7).

8. Tap the Post button. Your Shared Photo Stream is now created and an invitation to view it is sent to those you added in the To field. In the future, when you tap the Share button ( ), you can select this Shared Photo Stream to send additional photos to the same recipients.

FIGURE 5-8

Selecting Photo Stream photos in iPhoto

Create a Shared Photo Stream in iPhoto or Aperture

Mac users can quickly create a Shared Photo Stream using iPhoto or Aperture, Apple's two photo apps. They can select any photos in their library, even those not stored in their Photo Stream. There are several ways to share photos via Photo Stream in iPhoto and Aperture, including dragging and dropping a selection of images or creating a brand-new Shared Photo Stream from a selection of images.

1. Launch iPhoto or Aperture on your Mac and select the photos in your library that you want to add to your Shared Photo Stream, as Figure 5-8 shows.

2. Click the Share button ( ) at the bottom right of the window and click Photo Stream from the pop-over that appears.

3. Click New Photo Stream in the pop-over.

4. Enter the names or e-mail addresses of the people you want to share your Shared Photo Stream with in the To field of the pane that appears; if you type people's

names, iPhoto accesses your contacts to find their e-mail addresses.

5. Type a name for your Shared Photo Stream in the Name field.

6. Check the Public Website option if you want people to be able to view your Shared Photo Stream with a web browser (whether or not given an invitation). Otherwise, only those people who have iCloud accounts can view the Shared Photo Stream, on their iOS devices, Macs, or PCs.

7. Click the Share button ( ) to invite people to view your Shared Photo Stream.

Create a Shared Photo Stream on a PC

Without the benefit of iPhoto, PC users must use the iCloud control panel to share Photo Streams from their computer. You can find out how to install the iCloud control panel in Chapter 1. PC users also need to manually select the photos they want to share from a location on their computer.

1. Open a new Windows Explorer window (called File Explorer in Windows 8) and click Photo Stream from the Favorites section.

2. Click the New Photo Stream option.

3. Type the e-mail addresses of each person you want to share the Photo Stream with and enter a name for your shared stream in the Name field. Click Next.

4. Click the Choose Photos button and locate the photos you want to share on your computer's hard drive or storage media. When done, click the Open button.

5. Click Add a Comment for each image you want to add a caption to and type it into the field that appears.

6. Click Done to send the invites to your Shared Photo Stream.

You can also right-click an image in the Windows Explorer and choose Add to a Photo Stream in the contextual menu that appears. You are then asked whether to share that image with an existing Shared Photo Stream or to create a new Shared Photo Stream for that image.

Invite more people and remove subscribers from a Shared Photo Stream

Once you've sent invitations to a Shared Photo Stream, you're not limited to sharing your photos only with the people you selected initially. You can send more invitations at any time and you can remove subscribers from a Shared Photo Stream. You can edit Shared Photo Stream lists on an iPhone, iPad, or iPod Touch running iOS 6 or later or from a Mac or PC.

On an iOS device:

1. Launch the Photos app.
2. Go to the Photo Stream pane.
3. If you are using an iPhone or an iPod Touch, tap the blue arrow next to the name of the Shared Photo Stream you want to edit. iPad users tap the Edit button and then tap the Photo Stream they want to edit.
4. Tap the Add People button and enter the names or e-mail addresses of the people you want to add to the list of subscribers (shown in Figure 5-9). To remove people from the list, tap the name of the person you want to remove under Subscribers and then tap the Remove Subscriber button.

On a Mac:

1. Launch iPhoto.
2. Select Photo Stream from the Source list on the left of the window.
3. Select the Shared Photo Stream you want to edit and then click the Info button at the bottom of the window.
4. Click into the Shared With section after a name and begin typing a contact's name or e-mail address to enter a new subscriber. Click after a name and then

FIGURE 5-9

Editing Photo Stream subscribers

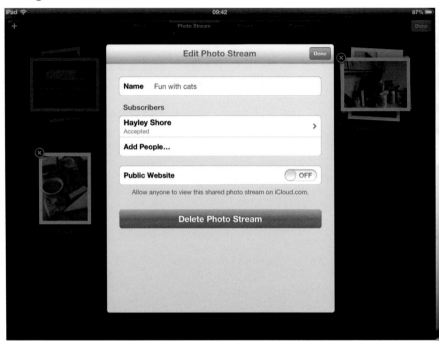

press Delete to remove a person as a subscriber (a confirmation settings sheet will appear to ask if you are sure).

On a Windows PC:

1. Open a new Windows Explorer window.
2. Choose Photo Stream from the Favorites section.
3. Double-click the Shared Photo Stream you want to edit and click Options in the window that appears.
4. Add subscribers by typing names or e-mail addresses in the list of subscribers and remove them by clicking the name of the subscriber you want to remove and clicking Remove. Click Done.

Viewing Shared Photo Streams shared by others

Of course, being an iCloud user, you can view Photo Streams that friends have invited you to view using your iOS device, Mac, or PC or via the web on any web-capable device.

You first need to be invited by someone sharing a Photo Stream. This invitation comes in the form of an e-mail or a notification that includes a subscribe link. Once you click the link or the Accept button, you are subscribed to the Shared Photo Stream.

The Shared Photo Stream appears in the Photo Stream section of the Photos app in your iOS device. In iPhoto or Aperture on your Mac, it also appears in the Photo Stream section. In Windows, you view the Shared Photo Stream by opening a new Windows Explorer window and clicking Photo Stream under Favorite Links.

If you aren't using any of these devices or don't have an iCloud account, you can view a Shared Photo Stream online (see Figure 5-10) if the person sharing the stream has turned

FIGURE 5-10

A Shared Photo Stream viewed on the web

on the Public Website setting for that Shared Photo Stream; if you were invited to the Shared Photo Stream, that invite will have a link to the web version. From a browser, you can view photos but not "like" or comment on them.

"Like" and comment on Shared Photo Stream photos

Similar to Facebook and other social networks, when you have access to a Shared Photo Stream, you can add comments to pictures or simply "like" them to apply your seal of approval. Comments and "likes" can be added to photos on an iOS device, Mac, or PC and you can even "like" photos via an iCloud-connected Apple TV. On all devices, you need to be viewing the photo you want to "like" or comment on to perform either function.

On iOS devices and in iPhoto on the Mac, a small speech bubble icon () appears below each Shared Photo Stream photo. Tapping or clicking the speech bubble allows you to add a comment or "like" the photo. On an Apple TV, you need to select the photo with the center button on the remote and then click again to "like" a photo. Clicking the center button one more time removes your "like." PC users must access the Photo Stream from the Favorites section in a Windows Explorer window and click Comments on a specific photo to "like" it or comment on it.

Share Photo Journals with the iPhoto App

It's my humble opinion that, if you're an iOS and iCloud user, you should use as many of Apple's own apps to fully take advantage of the services you get for free; in this case, Photo Stream. I'm not saying that other apps shouldn't get a look, as there are plenty of great applications for photo sharing in the App Store, some that even include iCloud support, but you really can't go far wrong if you use an app made by the same

FIGURE 5-11

Journals in the iPhoto app

folks who brought you the device you're using and the cloud services it accesses.

That's why I believe the iPhoto app for iOS is such a great tool, especially for iPad users. It offers advanced editing features, access to your Photo Stream photos, and — the best part — Photo Journals (shown Figure 5-11). Photo Journals is a quick and easy way to create and publish a gallery of your best snaps without touching a computer or writing a line of code.

If you want to create a website solely for sharing photos, put down the web design software and take a look at Photo Journals. It's brilliant! Not only do you get to drag and drop your pictures (see Figure 5-12), resize them, and share them with the world, you can add little widgets to the gallery as well. The widgets include calendar icons, text, quotes, maps (using information stored in the photos to pinpoint a location), and temperatures data, all laid out in a slick interface that anyone with a modern web browser can view. Clicking a photo in a Photo Journal expands it to a larger view from which viewers can then trigger a slideshow of the photos if they want.

And if you don't want to sit around plotting the perfect arrangement for your images, you can let iPhoto flow them into the Photo Journal automatically, so all you have to do is tap the Share button (⬈) or publish the journal to iCloud.

Each time you create a Photo Journal in iPhoto, you can send it to your iCloud home page where all your public Photo Journals are stored. Over time, you create a beautiful web gallery of your best images and make a brilliant way to show off your photography skills.

The iPhoto app isn't particularly pricey at $5, and if you're already using iCloud, it's a sensible choice to extend your photography experience on your iOS device, enabling you to share photos far better than before. It's also a good way to share photos if you're primarily dealing with friends and family who don't have iCloud accounts. Although they can't access Shared Photo Streams on their devices, they can access the web pages that contain a Photo Journal. And a Photo Journal frankly looks far more attractive than the web gallery pages created by Photo Stream.

Create and share a Photo Journal to iCloud

After you launch iPhoto on your iOS device, follow these steps:

1. Go to the Albums pane.
2. Select an album, tap the Share button (⬈), and tap Journal in the pop-over that appears.
3. Tap All to use all the photos in the album or tap Choose Photos to manually select the photos you want to use, then tap the Next button.
4. Add a title for your Photo Journal in the field provided and select a style from the options.

FIGURE 5-12

Creating journals in the iPhoto app

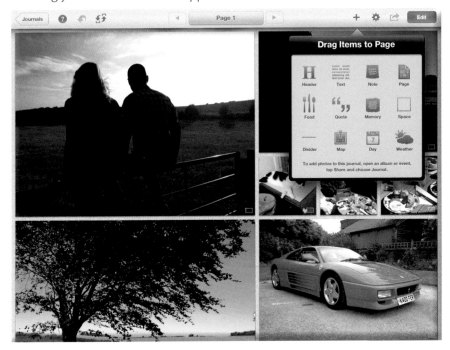

5. Tap the Create Journal button.
6. Tap the Show button on the alert that appears.
7. iPhoto automatically lays out your Photo Journal but you can make changes to the layout by tapping the Edit button and then tapping and holding an image until it becomes enlarged. You can now drag the image to a new location.
8. Double-tap an image while in Edit mode and use the handles that appear at the image's edge to resize an image.
9. Tap the Add button (the + icon) at the top of the screen to drag in a new widget item such as a header, note, or map (see Figure 5-12).
10. When you are done editing your Photo Journal, tap the Share button (📤) and choose iCloud from the menu that appears. Set the Publish to iCloud switch to On.

11. You now have the option to share your journal, view it in Safari, or add it to your iCloud home page.

Each time you make changes to your journal, be sure to tap the Publish Changes button to keep the web-based version up to date.

Send Photos via E-mail on an iOS Device

For a more "old school" way of sending photos with iCloud, you can always use good old e-mail. There are several ways to send a picture in an e-mail: You can create the e-mail first and then insert the picture into the e-mail by tapping and holding in the text and choosing Insert Photo or Video from the contextual menu that appears (a new capability in iOS 6), or you can choose the Mail option from the Share pop-over when viewing a picture or a group of pictures in the Photos app.

As long as you have a decent connection to a Wi-Fi or cellular data network, sending photos by e-mail is a quick and convenient method. Here are the easiest ways to share your pictures over e-mail.

To sending pictures via e-mail from the Photos app:

1. Select the album or Photo Stream that contains the photos you want to share.
2. Tap the Edit button and then tap each photo you want to share. A check mark will appear on all the selected photos. Note that if you select more than four, you won't be able to send them via e-mail, so if you have more than four photos to e-mail, you'll need to send the in batches.
3. Tap the Share button (↪) and choose Mail in the pop-over that appears.
4. The Mail app will appear with a new e-mail message, with the photos attached. Specify the recipients in the To field, type a subject, and add to the message body any other text you want.

5. Tap the Send button.

To add photos to an e-mail message you are composing in Mail:

1. Tap and hold in the message body to display the contextual menu.
2. Tap the Insert Photo or Video option (see Figure 5-13). On an iPhone or iPod Touch, you may have to scroll through the contextual menu by tapping the arrow buttons to see this option.
3. Select the photos you want to add to the e-mail and tap the Choose button.
4. When you're ready to send the e-mail, tap Send in Mail.

To copy and paste a photo into a new e-mail:

1. In the app displaying the photo you want to copy, tap and hold on the photo you want to send until the contextual menu appears. (Note that not all apps support copying of images; such apps won't display the contextual menu.)
2. Tap the Copy option.
3. Go to the Mail app.

FIGURE 5-13

The Insert Photo or Video option in the Mail app

4. Create a new e-mail and tap and hold in the body of the e-mail.
5. Tap Paste in the contextual menu that appears to add your photo to the e-mail.

Send Photos to Social Media Sites from an iOS Device

iOS 6 has baked-in support for both Facebook and Twitter, which makes it even easier to share your photos online so all your friends and followers can see them. Using such social networks to share your photos lets you reach more people more quickly, as you don't select the individual recipients as in an e-mail but simply send the photo to everyone monitoring your Twitter feed or Facebook posts.

To share via Twitter or Facebook, you need to have signed up to your account in the Settings app. Then, in the Photos app, tap the Share button ( ) to open the Share pop-over (the same one that has the Mail option). Facebook allows multiple photos to be uploaded whereas Twitter only lets you share one picture at a time. So if you select more than one photo, the Twitter option does not appear in the Share pop-over.

When you share via Facebook, you get a pop-over in which you enter a message to go with your photos. You also need to tap the album name below the photo preview to select a Facebook album to send the photos to. You can also add a location and set the Facebook Audience for your photos by tapping the respective links below the message area. Tap the Post button when done.

When you share via Twitter, you also get a pop-over in which you enter a message to go with your photo (see Figure 5-14). You can include a location by tapping Add Location. When done, tap Send to share your photo on Twitter.

FIGURE 5-14

Sharing a photo to Twitter

Store Images in Your Photo Stream

Sometimes, you want to add to your Photo Stream images and photos that you didn't take with your camera or got from your computer's Photo Stream (via iPhoto or Aperture on the Mac, and via the folders in Windows set for Photo Stream). On an iOS device, there are several ways to get images into Photo Stream as well.

Save images from websites in Safari

Many websites let you save their images locally, which is an easy way to get them into Photo Stream on your iOS device.

1. In Safari, browse to the website that contains the picture you want to save on your iOS device.

2. Locate the picture you want to save and tap and hold your finger on it until the contextual menu appears.

3. Tap Save Image to store the image in your iOS device's Photos app. It will reside in your Camera Roll album, as well as be placed into Photo Stream.

Take a screenshot on an iOS device

For websites that don't let you save their images, or to share images of your iOS device's screen (such as to show someone how to do something), use the screenshot feature in iOS to take a picture of the screen.

1. On your iOS device, open the app, website, or anything else you want to take a picture of.
2. Press the Home button and the Sleep/Wake button simultaneously.
3. The screen should flash white and you should hear the camera shutter sound (unless your device is muted). The screen image will reside in your Camera Roll album, as well as be placed into Photo Stream.

Assign a Photo to an iCloud Contact

The beauty of having all your contacts linked and in sync among devices with iCloud is that a change to a contact on one device is made to the same contact on all the others. One aspect of a contact is the ability to assign a photo to the person, so that photo appears on your iPhone screen when he or she calls you, for example, as Figure 5-15 shows.

You can take these photos easily on an iPhone and assign them to the contacts there, knowing that the photos are then available on your other iOS devices and computers (such as in e-mail message headers in your inbox on your computer). Of course, the image you assign to a person's contact card doesn't have to be an actual photo — you can use any image, as Figure 5-15 shows.

1. Select a photo in the Photos app and tap the Share button (⤴).

Whatever image you assign to a contact displays on your iPhone when that person calls you.

2. Tap the Assign to Contact option in the pop-over that appears, as Figure 5-16 shows.
3. Select the contact you want to assign the photo to from the list of contacts shown.

Adding a custom image to a contact in iOS. Left: The Share pop-over in Photos. Right: The screen in which you set the image and assign it.

4. Resize and crop the image as desired using the expand and pinch gestures (to resize) and scroll gesture (to crop), as Figure 5-16 shows.
5. Tap the Choose button to assign the image to the contact.

Stream Photos to a TV

Sending photos to the web or sharing them via e-mail is nowhere near as fun or personal as showing them off to friends and family in the comfort of your own home. If you have pictures on your iOS device or computer, you can simply hand the device to a friend or have them sit in front of your computer and flick through the photos, but even that's not taking full advantage of the features of iCloud and AirPlay. Adding an Apple TV to the mix makes things even better.

Just like the beautiful people in immaculate homes in the Apple advertisements, you too can share photos on your TV screen using the magic of AirPlay. The same principle applies to streaming photos as it does music and movies: You need a compatible device to send the media as well as a compatible device to receive it. In most cases, the device sending the pictures will be an iPhone, iPad, iPod Touch, or a computer and the receiver will be the Apple TV.

But you can access photos stored in your Photo Stream right from your Apple TV without having to send it from another device. When connected to your iCloud account, your Apple TV can pull photos from the web and display them on your TV very easily. It can also access the photos stored on your computer, too.

Display photos from an iOS device on an Apple TV

With your iOS device and Apple TV connected to the same network, you can quickly stream a photo to your TV's screen in a matter of taps. Your Apple TV and the TV it is connected to need to be switched on and you need to have photos in the Photos app on your iOS device.

1. Locate the photo you want to send in the Photos app on your iOS device.
2. Tap the photo to show it at full screen size and then tap the picture to display the toolbars at the top and bottom of your iOS device's screen.
3. Tap the AirPlay button (⌷) and choose your Apple TV from the list that appears.
4. The picture will appear on the TV connected to your Apple TV.
5. You can swipe across the image on your iOS device to show the next image in the current album on your Apple TV. Continue doing so to show more photos if you want.

Stream a slideshow of photos from an iOS device to an Apple TV

In the same way that you can send one photo to your Apple TV via AirPlay, you can send a slideshow on your iOS device to an Apple TV. Slideshows offer a more attractive way to stream a set of images. All you need to do is set the transition effect between images and set whether to play music during the slideshow — then you're good to go. (You will, of course, need to have music stored on your iOS device to play music during your slideshow.)

Unless you want your slideshow to be of every image on your iOS device (in the Camera Roll album) or in your Photo Stream (in the Photo Stream album), you should first create an album of the images you want to show in your slideshow. That's easy:

1. In the Photos app, open your Camera Roll or Photo Stream album, then tap Edit.
2. Now select each image you want to copy to a new album.

3. Tap the Save button and choose Save to New Album in the menu that appears.

4. Enter a name for the album and click Save in the dialog box that appears. The album now appears in the albums list in Photos.

To play a slideshow:

1. In the Photos app, select the album you want to create a slideshow from.

2. Tap the picture you want to use as the start of your slideshow; this makes it display in full screen. Now tap again to show the toolbars at the top and bottom of the interface.

3. Tap the AirPlay button (⬆) and select your Apple TV from the list that appears.

4. On an iPhone or iPod Touch, tap the Play button (▶) at the bottom of the screen. On an iPad, tap the Slideshow button at the top of the screen. The Slideshow Options window (on the iPhone or iPod Touch) or pop-over (on the iPad) appears (see Figure 5-17).

5. On the iPad only, you can select AirPlay in the Slideshow pop-over that appears, in case you forgot to enable AirPlay previously via the AirPlay button (⬆).

6. In the Slideshow Options pop-over, tap Transitions and select a transition effect from the list of options that appears.

7. If you want music during your slideshow, set the Play Music switch to On and select a song from your device's music library by tapping the Music option that appears.

8. When you're ready, tap the Start Slideshow button to begin streaming your slideshow to your Apple TV. The pictures will appear on the TV screen and, if you chose to play music too, it will play through the TV's speakers or your home entertainment system if you have one connected to your TV.

FIGURE 5-17

The Slideshow Options window in the Photos app

Give Presentations via AirPlay

The more business-focused among you may be looking at this photo-streaming technology as a useful route to giving presentations in an office or when visiting clients. You'd be right.

If your presentation is made up of photos and screenshots, making an album of these images is an easy way to create a quick presentation that you then stream from the Photos app to an Apple TV or through a video-out cable that connects your iOS device to a projector or TV. (Apple sells such cables with VGA and HDMI adapters.) Either way, you choose the output device via the AirPlay feature on your iOS device.

If you want to give traditional PowerPoint presentations, get the $10 Keynote app from Apple. It's a great tool for creating professional slideshows — complete with transitions and animations — on your iOS device, plus it opens Microsoft PowerPoint or Apple Keynote presentations created on a computer.

Using the joys of AirPlay mirroring, you are not only able to stream slides from your computer or iOS device to

FIGURE 5-18

The Keynote Remote app with presenter notes displayed

an Apple TV, but you can also control the slideshow and access additional controls and information from your iOS device's screen or from an additional display attached to your computer. Keynote provides a separate display for presenter notes that allows the presenter to view several elements including a timer and notes for each slide.

The free Keynote Remote app (shown in Figure 5-18) runs on any iOS device (though it's designed for the iPhone and iPod Touch) and remote-controls Keynote on a Mac or other iOS device. For example, if your presentation is on your iPad or Mac and you want to walk around the stage during your presentation, you would use Keynote Remote on your iPhone or iPod Touch to move through the slides and even read the presenter notes. Note that you need a Wi-Fi connection or Bluetooth connection between the iOS device running Keynote Remote and the iOS device or Mac that is running the presentation.

Access Your Photos on an Apple TV

An Apple TV can access photos stored on your computer and in your Photo Stream.

To access the photos on your computer, the Apple TV needs to be signed into the same Home Sharing account as the computer that has the photos, and iTunes needs to be running on that computer.

- Sign in to Home Sharing on the computer in iTunes by choosing File ⇨ Home Sharing ⇨ Turn Home Sharing On.
- On your Apple TV, go to the Settings screen, choose Computers, choose Turn On Home Sharing, and sign in with the same Home Sharing account as the computer uses.

To access the photos in your Photo Stream, the Apple TV needs to be signed into your iCloud account and Photo Stream needs to be enabled:

1. Go to the Settings screen on your Apple TV and choose iTunes Store from the menu. If no iCloud account appears, choose Sign In, enter your iCloud e-mail address, then click the Submit button. Enter your password, then click the Submit button.
2. Go to the Photo Stream screen on the Apple TV.
   - If you're not signed in to iCloud, you'll see the Photo Stream Setup screen, where you can choose to connect to the current iCloud account's Photo Stream or to sign in with an other account.
   - If you want to watch someone else's Photo Stream, scroll down and choose Settings, then choose Sign Out in the screen that appears. Go to the Photo Stream screen again and sign in to that other account. (That account will stay signed in until you sign out of it.)

Access photos stored on your computer on an Apple TV

To access iPhoto albums or any other photos stored on your computer via your Apple TV, first be sure you've signed into Home Sharing on both the computer and the Apple TV. In iTunes on your computer:

1. Choose File ⇨ Home Sharing ⇨ Choose Photos to Share with Apple TV.

2. In the window that appears, select the Share Photos option, then choose the source from the menu to its right. On a Mac, your options are iPhoto, Aperture (if you have this software installed), Choose Folder, and Pictures. In Windows, your options are Choose Folder and My Pictures.

   ○ If you choose iPhoto or Aperture, you get the options All Photos, Albums, Events, and Faces (this will display everything in iPhoto or Aperture on your Apple TV) and Selected Albums, Events, and Faces (this lets you choose what to share from a list that appears below). No matter which you choose, there's also the option Include Videos to let you decide whether to show just photos (deselect this option) or photos and videos (select this option).

   ○ If you choose Pictures or My Pictures, you also get two options for how much you want to share — All Folders and Selected Folders — as well as the Include Videos option to control whether videos are played as well. If you have no subfolders, the Selected Folders option is grayed out. If you select Selected Folders, a list of subfolders appears that you can then choose from (multiple selections are allowed). Think of each folder as an album; it's a good idea to organize your photos into subfolders ahead of time, so you don't accidentally show photos you didn't intend to.

   ○ If you choose Choose Folder, a settings sheet appears where you navigate to the folder on your computer that contains the photos you want to show. You get the same options here as you do when you choose Pictures or My Pictures.

3. Click Apply to permit the display of your photos on the Apple TV. Close the window.

4. On your Apple TV, open the Computers screen and choose the iTunes library for the computer you are sharing your photos from. (Multiple computers can use the same Home Sharing account.)

5. Select the Photos option. (You only see the Photos option if that computer is sharing photos.)

6. You'll see tiles for the available photos. Use the arrow buttons on the Apple TV control to navigate to a specific photo, then press the Enter button (the center button) to display that photo in full-screen view.

7. If you want the Apple TV to play back all the photos as a slideshow starting with the selected photo, press the Play button (▶).

8. Press Menu to go back to the tiles to select a different photo.

9. To stop sharing these photos with the Apple TV, go to iTunes on your computer and choose File ➪ Home Sharing ➪ Choose Photos to Share with Apple TV. In the window that appears, deselect the Share Photos option, click Apply, and close the window.

Access Photo Stream photos on an Apple TV

Once you're signed in via your iCloud account:

1. On the Apple TV, go to the Photo Stream screen by selecting the Photo Stream badge at the bottom of the list of services.

2. A screen appears showing your Photo Stream and any Shared Photo Streams you are subscribed to. Select the desired Photo Stream to view it.

3. You'll see tiles for the available photos. Use the arrow buttons on the Apple TV control to navigate to a specific photo, then press the Enter button (the center button) to display that photo in full-screen view.
4. If you want the Apple TV to play back all the photos as a slideshow starting with the selected photo, press the Play button (▶).
5. Press Menu to go back to the tiles to select a different photo.

Play Photo Stream photos or iPhoto albums as a slideshow on an Apple TV

The basic slideshow playback capability on the Apple TV is nice, but it can do more than that. When viewing photos shared from a computer or from a Photo Stream, note the Slideshow button at the top of the Apple TV's screen.

1. Select the Slideshow button at the top of the screen using the Enter button on the Apple TV's remote control.
2. Scroll down and select the Shuffle Photos setting if you want your photos to display in random order.
3. Go to the Repeat Photos section. Set this option to On if you want the slideshow to keep repeating; set it to Off to have the slideshow run through the images just once.
4. If you want music to play during the slideshow, select Default Music to pick a playlist or entire collection of songs from your iTunes library or from your iTunes Match library. (Set the option to None so no music plays during your slideshow.)
5. If you want to change the theme for the slideshow's transitions, scroll down to the Themes section and select a theme from the list. A preview of the selected theme appears behind the Slideshow Settings screen so

you can get a feel for the style you have chosen before committing to it.

A DAY IN THE LIFE: PHOTOS THAT SHARE MEMORIES

It's the weekend and you're spending a day out with friends. As you enjoy a good walk in the country you snap photos of the sights and scenes on your iPhone. Over a hearty lunch, you use your iPad to show off your photos that have synced via Photo Stream to your iPad to friends around the table.

Several say they'd love to see the images later on. Without flinching, you create a Shared Photo Stream from all the photos you have taken that day and invite your iCloud-using friends to subscribe to it then and there They all do and even begin commenting and "liking" the pictures you've posted. One of your friends doesn't use iCloud, so you invite her by making sure that a public site is created for the Photo Stream so she can access the pictures through a web browser.

You also upload a few of the photos to Facebook with a link to the public Photo Stream page so other friends can check out the photos online.

After lunch, you head back to your place to meet a few more friends who want to hear all about your day. Rather than simply explain, you turn on your TV and access the Shared Photo Stream you created earlier via your Apple TV.

As people enjoy drinks, you start up a playlist via your iPhone and stream it to your Apple TV. After a few minutes, your screen saver turns on and shows your most recent Photo Stream photos, which includes the pictures you took that day.

After dinner and with even more photos taken, you settle down with your iPad and access the photos you took in the iPhoto app so you can create a Photo Journal for your friends to enjoy online and remember the great day you had.

6. When you're happy with your settings, scroll to the top of the menu and select Start Slideshow to begin playing the slideshow.

The settings you choose for your slideshow will remain in place for all future slideshows until you change them. Thus, after setting your preferred slideshow options, you just need to press the Play button (▶) to use them in other slideshows.

Set Photo Stream photos or iPhoto albums as an Apple TV screen saver

If you're a regular Apple TV user and have it connected to your TV and switched on a lot of the time, a screen saver is a great way to show off your photos. Normally, the Apple TV displays from a set of images that Apple included in the Apple TV, but you can have it use your Photo Stream photos or photos shared from your computer via Home Sharing instead.

1. On the Apple TV, go to the Settings screen.
2. Select the Screen Saver option.
3. Select the Photos option in the Screen Saver screen.
4. Scroll down and select either Photo Stream or the iTunes library for the computer that has shared photos. (That computer must be on and running iTunes for the Apple TV to see it.) If you select an iTunes library, you can choose any of the albums, folders, or events that you made available for sharing in iTunes.
5. Click Menu to return to the Screen Saver screen and select any other display options you want, such as the screen saver effects, how long the Apple TV must be idle before the screen saver displays, and whether the screen saver appears while the Apple TV is playing music from iTunes Match, an iOS device, or an iTunes library.
6. Select Preview to see how your settings will appear.
7. Press Menu to apply the changes.

TIP: Using the screen saver with appropriate images when playing music on the Apple TV is a great way to liven a party. For example, you might play a Christmas music playlist and display family photos from previous Christmases when people visit for the holidays. Or you might play a person's favorite music and show childhood images during a birthday party.

6

Stay in Touch

So, YOUR PHOTOS AND MOVIES ARE AVAILABLE ON ALL YOUR devices and are synced perfectly, but what about the more functional parts of your digital life? The contacts you need to get in touch with friends, family, and work colleagues? The e-mail and instant message conversations you want to keep going wherever you are? That's what this chapter will cover as well as entertaining features of iCloud and iOS such as using Location Services to find people and places and even connect to your computer at home.

It's tough to really understand just how useful it is to have all your contacts and e-mails in sync until you are caught without a vital phone number or message at a crucial time. At that point, of course, it's too late.

Check Your Connections

Before I delve into the ins and outs of editing and syncing contacts, you need to ensure that the same iCloud syncing for music, movies, and photos is also happening with your contacts. As with everything iCloud, a quick trip to the iCloud settings on all your devices should ensure that all works well.

A quick way to test your contact and mail syncing is to make changes on one device and see if they update in all your others. Any simple edit like deleting a Mail message or updating contact information should be the way to go. These changes should then be sent to the iCloud servers and pushed down to all your iCloud-connected devices in a matter of minutes, if not sooner — assuming the devices are connected to the Internet, of course.

You can accelerate the process in an iOS device's Contacts app by going to the Groups section and tapping the Refresh button (↻). In the Mail app on an iOS device, you can do the same by going to you iCloud e-mail account's inbox and then dragging down from the top and then letting go.

If the changes don't appear on one or more of your devices, check that they are connected to the Internet and signed in to the iCloud account you want to sync with.

Use Contacts with iCloud

It's often the case that an iCloud user creates an account and then finds duplicates or out-of-date contacts in the Contacts app on his or her iCloud-connected devices. To avoid such confusion and disorganization, it may be worth cleaning out your contact list entirely — adding missing contacts, deleting obsolete ones, and finding duplicates that you reconcile into one entry — and starting from scratch. It's easiest to so on a computer where you can more accurately see the contacts being synced and simply delete those you don't want.

The reason you likely have multiple contacts is that you have — or had — them stored in multiple lists. Before there ever was an iCloud, you probably had contacts on your Mac or PC, stored locally in its contacts application. And you may have synced them via iTunes to your iPhone or other iOS device, creating a copy. When you enabled iCloud, those contacts may not all have been moved to the iCloud list, so some don't sync across all your devices. Others may have been copied to iCloud from different devices, causing multiple copies in iCloud. Some may have been copied to iCloud but also kept in a local list on your computer, again causing duplicates to appear on some devices.

After you have cleaned up your contacts on your computer, move them all to iCloud so iCloud has the master list to sync with all other devices.

On a Mac:

1. Open the Contacts application (called Address Book in OS X 10.7 Lion) and select any contact.
2. Select all the contacts by pressing ⌘+A.
3. Drag the selected contacts into the All iCloud list at the left side of the Contacts application. This adds them to the iCloud group that ensures iCloud syncs them with all your other iCloud-connected devices.

In Windows:

1. Go to the iCloud control panel and turn off Contacts, wait a few seconds, and then turn it back on to see if this resolves the issue of not all contacts being in iCloud.

2. If not, make sure that the iCloud connector is enabled in Outlook 2007 or 2010:

   ○ In Outlook 2010, go to the File tab, click Options to open the Outlook Options window, and click Add-Ins to see which add-ins are enabled. Make sure iCloud Outlook Add-in is listed under Active Application Add-ins.

   ○ In Outlook 2007, choose Tools ➪ Trust Center and click Add-ins from the left column. Make sure iCloud Outlook Add-in is listed under Active Application Add-ins.

3. If the add-in is not installed, reinstall iCloud on your PC; you can download it from www.icloud.com/icloudcontrolpanel.

Keep Contacts up to date anywhere

With your contacts list up to date, you should see the same list of contacts on all your devices connected to iCloud. And changes on any one device should be reflected on all the others.

Editing or adding a contact is as simple as launching the Contacts app on a Mac or iOS device or, if you are a Windows user, the Microsoft Outlook app (version 2007 or later), then editing, removing, or adding contact information.

You can also go to www.icloud.com and sign in using your iCloud account information. Then open the Contacts app to view and manage the contacts stored in iCloud. Whatever contacts are shown at iCloud.com are the ones that iCloud knows about and will keep synced.

TIP: If you use a Microsoft Exchange or Google Gmail e-mail account, or a Google Contacts account, contacts stored there stay synced as well across all your devices connected to those accounts. But it's not iCloud that does the syncing; it's Exchange or Google. The notion is the same as iCloud syncing, just using their own services. If you want to import those contacts into iCloud, use the export function in those services (check their documentation) to create a vCard file that you can then import into Contacts on your Mac or Outlook on your PC. Or e-mail yourself the vCard file and open it on an iOS device to import it into your Contacts app there.

Some mobile phones and other devices store contact information on their SIM card. So if you move from another phone to an iPhone or cellular-capable iPad using the same SIM card, you can import these contacts into the Contacts app on your new device, and thus into iCloud:

1. Open the iOS Settings app and tap Mail, Contacts, Calendars.
2. Scroll until you see the Import SIM Contacts button and tap it.
3. Select where to import the contacts to (iCloud is of course the best option) — and you're done.

Enhance contact information for Siri

The Siri service on recent-model iPhones and iPads can be wonderful, letting you search for information, ask questions, and control some aspects of your iOS device all through voice queries and commands.

One aspect of Siri that you may overlook is its ability to associate people in your contacts list with their relationship to you, which can make using Siri that much easier. For example, "call Dad" or "locate my girlfriend."

Siri does this by using the relationships you set in your own contacts card, as Figure 6-1 shows:

1. Launch the Settings app and tap Mail, Contacts, Calendars.

2. Scroll down to Contacts and tap the My Info section to show the contact card Siri is currently using as yours. You can change the contact if you want.

3. Open the Contacts app, then select the contact card listed in the My Info section in the Settings app. It will have a silhouette of a head next to it as well as be in blue.

4. Tap the Edit button.

5. Scroll down until you see the Add Field option; tap it and then in the pop-over scroll down and tap Related People.

FIGURE 6-1

Adding family information to a contact card in Contacts

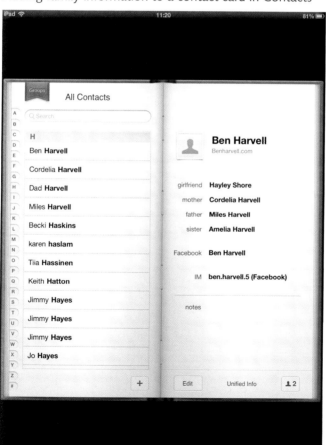

SHARE CONTACTS WITH A BUMP

Bump Technologies has come up with a pretty zany way to share information via your iOS device. With the Bump app installed, you can send contacts, photos, videos, and more to anyone using Bump by, you guessed it, bumping your devices together.

Brilliantly, the app works across a number of devices, so you can share with iPhone, iPad, and iPod Touch users as well as other smartphone types that support Bump. So now, bumping into someone in the street has a whole new meaning!

Even if you don't have friends to bump with, you can still quickly send pictures to your computer from your iOS device by bumping the spacebar with it. It's quirky, crazy, but undeniably clever.

6. The Mother field appears; tap the adjacent field to select your mother's contact card, or tap Mother to get a list of other relationships to use instead.
7. After you add a related person, a new relationship field appears below it (usually Mother or Father) that you use to add a second relationship.
8. Keep adding relevant relationships, one at a time.
9. Tap the Done button to save your changes.

It's worth filling out your personal information as fully as possible as it can help improve other Siri experiences, too, such as reminders. Asking Siri to remind you about something when you leave home or arrive at work, for example, is another good use of this feature (Siri will know what "home" or "work" means if you have those addresses listed in your contact card).

Thanks to the magic of iCloud, this Siri-helping information gets synced to your other devices, including those that have Siri.

Integrate Facebook contacts

Facebook integration, added in iOS 6, allows you to quickly share photos, videos, links, and posts to Facebook via the Share button (↰) that appears throughout iOS and its apps. By simply adding your Facebook account in the Settings app on an iOS device, you get this sharing and can receive updates through the Facebook app and in the iOS Notification Center.

Another handy trick that Facebook integration allows is the ability to keep your iCloud contacts updated with Facebook, essentially matching the contacts stored in iCloud with your friends on Facebook and making changes to the iCloud contact information when a friend changes their information on Facebook. It will even update your friends' pictures in the Contacts app if they change their Facebook profile picture.

Other information pulled from Facebook by apps on your iOS device includes Game Center profiles and birthdays in Calendar:

1. Launch the Settings app, scroll down to the Facebook label, and tap it to open the Facebook pane, shown in Figure 6-2.
2. If you haven't yet signed into Facebook, do so here. You can also download the Facebook app from this pane.
3. Turn on all the apps you want to allow access to your Facebook account using the switches next to each app. (Apps that connect to Facebook may ask you for permission to do so when you run them or try to share

FIGURE 6-2

Facebook settings in the Settings app

to Facebook from them; any you give permission to do so are also listed here.)

4. Tap the Update All Contacts option to sync your iCloud contacts with your Facebook friends. Do this periodically to keep iCloud contacts in sync with your Facebook contacts.

TIP: No sooner than Facebook integration was added to iOS that people noticed an annoying problem regarding e-mails and their contacts. Because most Facebook accounts feature an @facebook.com e-mail address by default, that e-mail address is added to your iCloud contacts when you sync contacts with Facebook. Many users don't use those

@facebook.com e-mail accounts, but because they got added to iCloud, those e-mail addresses started being used in Mail, often unintentionally. The result: E-mails that no one saw. To make sure that your friends don't get your @facebook.com e-mail address when they sync to Facebook on their iOS devices, go to your Facebook account on the web and hide your @facebook.com e-mail address in the Contact Info screen. (Go to the Contact Info section of your Facebook profile, click the Edit button, and set the privacy setting for your @facebook.com e-mail address to Only Me while making your main e-mail address visible to friends or the public. Ask your Facebook friends to do the same in their accounts.

Text and Video-Chat

Your mobile phone carrier provides SMS texting service for your iPhone, either for a monthly fee or a per-message charge. iCloud provides its own messaging service called iMessage that costs you nothing. And iMessage works on Macs, iPod Touches, and iPads, too — not just iPhones. And your iMessage conversations are available on all your devices, so you can start a conversation on an iPhone but continue it later in your iPad, for example. The only limitation is that it works just with other iCloud users who've enabled iMessage on their devices.

iCloud also lets you do video chats among iOS devices and Macs via the FaceTime app. (To video-chat with Windows users, you'll need to use the Skype app instead.)

Enable iMessage

On an iPhone, the Messages app handles both SMS and iMessage conversations (SMS messages have a green background, whereas iMessage ones have a blue bacground.) Other iOS devices's Messages apps handle just iMessage conversations, while Macs' Message app handles iMessage and a variety of other instant-messaging services such as AOL

An iMessage conversation in the iPad's Messages app

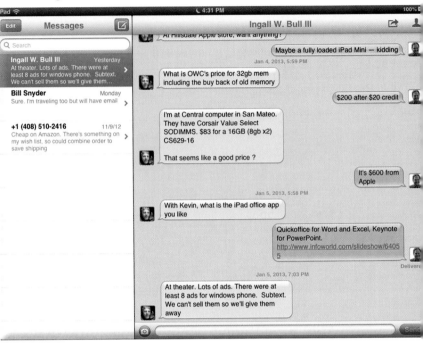

Instant Messenger (AIM), Google Talk, Jabber, and Yahoo. Figure 6-3 shows an iMessage conversation on the iPad.

As wonderful as iMessage is, it's not on by default. But it's not hard to turn on.

On an iOS device, go to the Settings app and open the Messages pane. Set the iMessage switch to On. Tap Send & Receive to specify which e-mail addresses people can use to find you for iMessage — if a person enters one of those e-mail addresses in your contacts card on his or her iOS device or Mac, the Messages app will know you have iMessage enabled and send the text to you that way, rather than via SMS. You also need to enter your Apple ID, which is how iCloud knows to keep your conversations synced across all your devices.

To ensure that you never send texts via SMS, slide the Send as SMS switch to Off. That prevents you from sending any texts to non-iMessage users. The Messages app always sends texts to iMessage users via iMessage, so you don't need to set Send as SMS to Off to ensure you don't waste money sending these people SMS texts.

To use Messages on a Mac, choose Messages ⇨ Preferences, go to the Accounts pane, click the Add button (the + icon), choose iMessage, and enter your Apple ID and the e-mail addresses and phone number you want people to be able to send your iMessage texts through.

TIP: iMessage is not the only messaging game in town, of course. The free Trillian service is available for Windows, iOS, Android, BlackBerry, and Mac OS X — and it's free. Trillian supports AIM, iCloud, Google Talk, Yahoo, Windows Live Messenger, and more as well as social network accounts like Facebook and Twitter. Like Messages, it keeps your conversations synced across all your devices.

Enable FaceTime

With an iCloud account, your FaceTime video conversations are available on any iOS device or Mac via the FaceTime app. Like iMessage, FaceTime taps into your contacts to connect to users who have FaceTime available. You can set favorite contacts that are then synced via iCloud to all your FaceTime devices.

FaceTime can be quickly set up on an iOS device and should be automatically installed and set up on a Mac when you add an iCloud account.

To set up FaceTime on an iOS device:

1. Launch the Settings app and tap the FaceTime label to open the FaceTime pane.
2. Set the FaceTime switch to On, as shown in Figure 6-4.
3. Tap the Use Your Apple ID for FaceTime button to enter your sign-in credentials. Enter your Apple ID information in the fields that appear and tap the Sign In button.
4. If you are using an iPhone, your phone number is displayed and all e-mail addresses associated with

FIGURE 6-4

Turning on FaceTime in the Settings app

your iCloud account are also shown. Deselect any that you don't want people to be able to find you at for a FaceTime conversation. (Any e-mail address listed can be used by the other person to initiate a FaceTime chat with you in their FaceTime app.) Tap Add Another Email to add an e-mail address not listed that you want people to be able to find you through.

5. If your cellular carrier supports FaceTime chats, you'll see the Use Cellular Data switch. Set it to On to be able to have chats over your data plan (note that these video chats can use a lot of data); if set to Off, you can use FaceTime only when connected to the Internet via a Wi-Fi connection.

On a Mac:

1. Launch the FaceTime application.
2. If you're not already signed in, your Apple ID is filled in but you need to enter your password in the field that displays and then click Sign In. You can also enter a different Apple ID and password to sign in from a

different account. Click Create New Account if you don't already have an Apple ID.

TIP: If you or your friends use a Windows PC, Android device, or Windows Phone, you can't use FaceTime to video-chat — it's an Apple-only technology. So you should use the free Skype service instead, as it is available for Mac, Windows, iOS, Windows Phone, and Android.

Use Skype as Your Universal Phone

You can use Skype (shown in Figure 6-5) as your main communication method across all your devices. The service isn't limited to just Skype-to-Skype calls, either. For an additional fee, you can use Skype to have calls with people's landline and cellular phones. If you call foreign numbers regularly, using Skype could be cheaper than a standard landline or cellular contract. With its paid service options, Skype can be used just like a regular phone with the added

FIGURE 6-5

Skype on a Mac

benefit that the same number can be used wherever you are. Just be aware that you can't call emergency numbers such as 911 or 999.

To further enhance your Skype experience, you can connect all your telephony devices — landline, Skype, and iPhone — to one device to control all incoming and outgoing calls. My favorite collection is the Plantronics Calisto Series. Offering traditional handsets, Bluetooth headsets, and speakerphones, these devices connect via Bluetooth to an iPhone, via USB to a computer, and via a standard phone line to a handset to provide complete control of all your telephony options. Whether you receive a call via Skype, your iPhone, or standard phone line, the call comes to the Calisto when it is turned on and in range, so you can pick it up from your Calisto handset, headset, or speakerphone as desired.

The Calisto devices also let you make outgoing calls through any of your telephony service — landline, Skype, or iPhone — and use common phone features such as speed dial and speakerphone. The Calisto handset and speakerphone also can show the caller ID on their LED screen, again regardless of the source of the call.

A cheaper alternative to Calisto, although not quite as feature-packed, is a Bluetooth headset that connects to your computer or your iOS device for receiving and making calls. You probably already have one for your iPhone for use in your car. As an added bonus, you can use Siri when the Bluetooth headset is connected to your iPhone so you can make calls with voice commands.

Get Local with Location Services

Using either GPS data or information from Wi-Fi hotspots, the Location Services capability pinpoints the location of your iOS device or Mac. There are several benefits to knowing your location:

- ⊙ It helps locate a missing iOS device using the Find My iPhone service.

- It can help you find where a friend is, if that person is using the free Find My Friends app and has consented to you tracking his or her location.
- It helps map and navigation apps show you where you are and route you to your desired location.
- It tags your photos with the location so you can remember just where you took them later.
- It lets you append location information to social networking services such as when you want to let people know where that great restaurant you just visited is.

It's worth noting that Location Services uses a lot of battery power, so when it's used extensively, such as for navigation, you should keep your device connected to a power source if at all possible.

When you set up your iOS device, you were asked whether you wanted Location Services enabled. But you can always turn it off via the Settings app, a well as manage which apps have access to your location information:

1. Launch the Settings app, and tap the Privacy label to open the Privacy pane.
2. Tap Location Services.
3. Set the Location Services switch to On (as shown in Figure 6-6).
4. Scroll through the list of apps that can access Location Services and set the switches to On or Off according to your preference.

On a Mac:

1. Choose ⇨ System Preferences to open the System Preferences application.
2. Go to the Security & Privacy system preference.
3. Click the lock icon at the lower left of the window and enter your account login information (or an administrator's credentials) so you can make changes to this system preference.
4. Go to the Privacy pane and click Location Services in the list at left.

FIGURE 6-6

Turning on Location Services and adjusting individual apps' permissions for your location information in the Settings app

5. Select Enable Location Services to turn on Location Services, or deselect the option to turn it off.
6. A list of apps that use your location appear in the pane at right; deselect any that you don't want to track your location.
7. Quit System Preferences when done.

Set up Find My iPhone

Although the service is called Find My iPhone, it can be used to find any of your iOS devices, including iPhones, iPads, and iPod Touches, as well as Macs. Location Services needs to be on in each device, as does the Find My iPhone/iPad/iPod/Mac.

On an iOS device:

1. Launch the Settings app and tap the iCloud label to open the iCloud pane.
2. Set the Find My iPhone switch to On. (It will be called Find My iPad on an iPad and Find My iPod on an iPod Touch.)

On a Mac:

1. Launch System Preferences and go to the iCloud system preference.
2. Make sure you are signed in to your iCloud account and that the Find My Mac option is selected.
3. Quit System Preferences when done.

Locate devices with Find My iPhone

If your device has been lost or stolen, you may be able to find it, thanks to iCloud. As long as the device is switched on and connected to the Internet (your Mac must have Wi-Fi turned on) and Find My iPhone/iPad/iPod/Mac has been set up on the device, you should be able to locate it using either the iCloud website (www.icloud.com) or the free Find My iPhone app on another device. In either case, you log in via your Apple ID or iCloud account.

From iCloud.com:

1. Click Find My iPhone.
2. Click the Devices button at the top of the window, then select a device from the Devices pop-over that appears. Or click a green bubble that appears on the map to see what device it is; nearby devices display here until you select a device in the Devices pop-over.
3. If you select a device from the Devices pop-over, controls for that device appear at the upper right of the window, as Figure 6-7 shows. To see these controls

FIGURE 6-7

Finding an iPhone via iCloud.com

for a device that you select on the map, click the *i* button next to the device's name.

From the Find My iPhone app:

1. On an iPhone or iPod Touch, tap on the device you want to locate, or tap All Devices. A map appears showing the device's or devices' location. On an iPad, tap the Devices button to open a pop-over from which you select the device you are trying to find (see Figure 6-8), or tap the All Devices button to see all devices; either way, the selected device or devices appear on the map.

2. If you tapped All Devices, tap the green bubble for a device to see what it is; tap the *i* button to open the controls for that device. If you selected a single device on the iPad, the controls appear automatically at

FIGURE 6-8

Choosing a device to locate with Find My iPhone on an iPad

the upper right of the screen. If you selected a single device on the iPhone or iPod Touch, tap the More button (⊙) to display the controls at the bottom of the screen.

3. Use the control buttons at the bottom of the screen to perform actions on the device, including playing a sound, locking the device, or erasing its data. (Playing a sound is handy if you suspect it's under a cushion or pile of papers in your home, for example.)

Use the Find My Friends app

The free Find My Friends app, shown in Figure 6-9, works in a similar way to the Find My iPhone app, except it allows you to track the location of people you know rather than your devices. If you are using the Find My Friends app, you can also broadcast your location so that friends know where you are.

It may sound a little dangerous to be letting the world know where you happen to be at any time but, because the app relies on an invite system, you can be safe knowing that only those you have allowed access to your location via Find My Friends can see where you are. Plus, you can always stop sharing your location in the app, or turn off Location Services completely if you want.

Privacy fears aside, there are real benefits to using Find My Friends with your close friends and family. First, you could use it when attending a sports match, concert, or any other major event where you're likely to be spread out over a large area. Second, the app makes it easier to meet up with people in a new location rather than have them give you directions. The app is also very useful for those who work at home to get a handle on when a partner is headed home from the office so you can put the kettle on or put some effort into making it look like you've been working hard all day. For these situations, you can set the app to alert you when a contact arrives at or leaves a specific location, and you can send alerts to others when you do the same.

Find My Friends doesn't come preinstalled on iOS devices, so has to be downloaded from the App Store. Once downloaded and installed, you need to log in with your iCloud username and password, and then invite others to use the app so you can see their location and they can see yours. Find My Friends can also access your contacts to suggest people to invite who are already using the app.

1. Tap the Friends button at the bottom of the screen to display your friends and their current locations.
2. To add a friend, tap the Add button (the + icon) at the top of the screen.
3. In the dialog box that appears, enter the name or e-mail address of the person you want to invite in the To field. Add a message if you want as well. Then tap Send.
4. You can also use the Friend Suggestions button in that dialog box to get a list of people from your contacts list

FIGURE 6-9

The Find My Friends app

who are already using the app, so you can send them invitations.

5. When a person accepts your invite, his or her location appears on the map on the Friends screen, and you'll see an entry for that person in your Friends list.

When you're meeting friends and family at a large event, it can be handy to share your location for a period of time so you can see when people arrive and where they are, especially if you're outdoors or in a crowd. In the Find My Friends app, you can invite contacts to temporarily share locations for a set period, after which locations will not be shared.

1. Tap the Temporary button at the bottom of the screen.
2. Tap the Invite Friends button.
3. Enter e-mail addresses or contact names in the To field and add a name for the event you will be attending in the Name field.

4. Tap the Ends field and select a date and time for location sharing to end.

5. Tap the Send button to invite friends to temporarily share their location.

To be notified when a friend arrives at or leaves a location:

6. In the Find My Friends app, tap the Friends button at the bottom of the screen.

7. Tap the name of a friend from the list next to the map and then tap the Notify Me button (at the top of the screen on the iPhone and iPod Touch, and at the bottom right on the iPad).

8. In the window that appears, tap Leaves to be notified when a friend leaves his or her current location. Tap Arrives to be notified when a friend arrives at a location, tap Arrives. Specify the location you want to be notified about by tapping the field below Arrives; you'll see My Current Location as an option, as well

FIGURE 6-10

Hiding your location from followers in the Find My Friends app

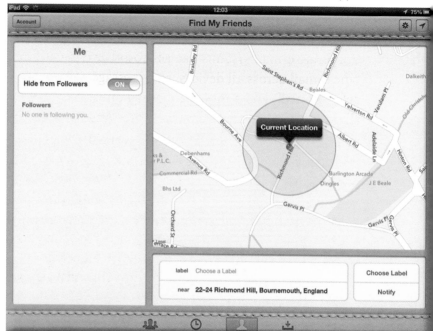

as any addresses for that person in your contacts. Tap Enter an Address to specify another location.

If you want to temporarily stop sharing your location through Find My Friends:

1. Tap the Me button at the bottom of the screen.
2. Set the Hide from Followers setting to On (see Figure 6-10).

E-mail Wherever You Are

Making sure you have access to e-mail is always important. Using iCloud or several other e-mail services, you can keep your e-mail accounts in sync and available across all your devices. iCloud e-mail should be up and running already if you set up your iOS device with an iCloud account but, if not, it's quick and easy to add your iCloud e-mail to an iOS device, Mac, or PC, or to access it online. PC users need to be using Microsoft Outlook 2007 or later to access iCloud e-mail or, alternatively, they can access their mail through a browser by visiting iCloud.com.

You might wonder what the big deal is about keeping e-mail up to date on multiple devices — "isn't that how it works?" you may be asking. The answer is "yes, sometimes." Corporate e-mail systems like Microsoft Exchange do in fact sync e-mail across all devices, so a message deleted on one is deleted on all, and a message read on one is still available to all others. Folders are kept synced, too. And some personal e-mail accounts do the same, if they use a protocol called IMAP. But many of the e-mail services you get from your Internet service provider or other free sources use a protocol called POP that doesn't sync e-mail across multiple devices (nor support folders) — that's a recipe for e-mail confusion.

The free iCloud e-mail account you get with a Mac or iOS device uses IMAP, ensuring that your e-mail is kept in sync. Thus, it's a great service to use for your standard personal e-mail instead of some other free account.

FIGURE 6-11

The iCloud system preference on a Mac

Apple makes it easy to use iCloud on iOS devices, Macs, and Windows PCs:

- ◎ In iOS, go to the Settings app, go to the iCloud pane.
- ◎ On a Mac, open the iCloud system preference (see Figure 6-11).
- ◎ On a Windows PC, open the iCloud control panel.

In all three cases, make sure your iCloud account is active, and set the Mail switch to On. If you're asked for your password, enter it.

You can also go to www.icloud.com via a web browser, sign in, and click the Mail icon to access your iCloud e-mail, create new messages, delete messages, and so on.

Set an out-of-office message for iCloud mail

If you're not going to be able to access your e-mails when you're out of the office or away on vacation, you can set the iCloud.com website to automatically respond to incoming e-mails with a custom message. These replies will continue to be sent until you turn the auto-response off.

After signing into your account at the iCloud.com website:

1. Click Mail.

SYNC CONTACTS AND CALENDARS WITH ANDROID

You can also access your iCloud e-mail account from an Android device. When configuring a new e-mail account, add the @me.com version of your address — not the @icloud.com version — as the e-mail address. The incoming server is mail.me.com, and SSL should be on. The outgoing server is smtp.me.com, TLS should be enabled, and you need to require sign-in using your @me.com address as the username and your standard iCloud password for the password. And if you want to sync your iCloud contacts with Android, get the $4 SmoothSync for Contacts Android app; likewise, to sync your iCloud calendar with Android, get the $4 SmoothSync for Calendar Android app.

2. Click the Settings button (✿) and choose Preferences from the pop-up menu that appears.
3. Click the Vacation button to go to the Vacations pane.
4. Check the box next to Auto-response and enter the response to be sent in reply to any incoming e-mail.
5. Click the Done button.

When you return from your absence, sign in to iCloud.com, repeat Steps 1 through 3, deselect the Auto-response option, and click Done.

Use iCloud e-mail forwarding

The iCloud.com website also allows you to forward incoming messages to a different address, such as to a colleague or family member handling your messages while you are absent.

After signing into your account at the iCloud.com website:

1. Click the Mail button.
2. Click the Settings button (✿) and choose Preferences from the pop-up menu that appears.

FIGURE 6-12

Forwarding e-mail from iCloud.com

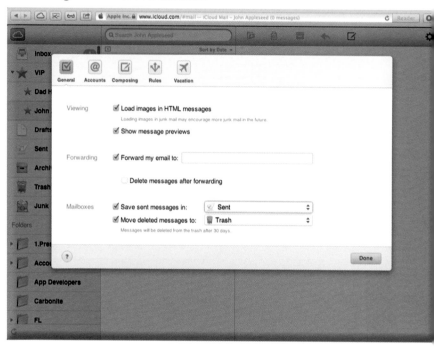

3. In the General pane, select the Forward My Email To option and enter the e-mail address you want to forward the messages to (shown in Figure 6-12).

4. If you want the original messages deleted from your account (a risky option as they'll no longer be available for reference), also select the Delete Messages after Forwarding option.

5. Click the Done button.

When you return from your absence, sign in to iCloud.com, repeat Steps 1 and 2, deselect the Forward My Email To option, and click Done.

Set iCloud mail rules

You probably use mail rules on your computer, such as to move messages from specific people or with specific subject text into folders — and of course to handle spam. You can't do that on an iOS device, and any rules you set on your computer apply only when the computer checks e-mail. The more mobile you are, the less your computer may be on to process those rules on your iCloud e-mail.

But you can set up these rules at the iCloud.com site, so they are applied to your e-mail before it reaches your devices or computers.

After signing into your account at the iCloud.com website:

A Day in the Life: Contacts, Messages, and E-mail

You're going on vacation with a group of friends. Before you leave the office and head for the airport, you log in to your iCloud.com account and set an out-of-office auto reply to let people know when you'll be back and that you won't be checking your e-mail as often while you sip margaritas on the beach.

You're meeting friends at the airport check-in, so you fire off an invite to them all to share their location on Find My Friends, so you know how far away from the airport they all are. You arrive first and see that your friends are nearing the car park, so you quickly share your location so they can find you in the terminal.

When you arrive at your vacation destination, you see an e-mail from a work colleague that needs immediate attention. Using the hotel's Wi-Fi, you get in touch via iMessage and set up a good time to talk. On his way to work, your colleague calls you via FaceTime and you brief him, face to face, on a meeting that's coming up.

While looking out at the island from a scenic viewpoint, a new iMessage arrives from your colleague: He clinched the deal. While you Skype with him on the bus ride back, you decide that he should deal with incoming e-mails so you can get on with your holiday, so you access your iCloud account at iCloud.com in the hotel lobby that night and forward all incoming e-mails to his work e-mail address.

You then shut off your devices and enjoy the sun.

1. Click the Mail button.
2. Click the Settings button (⚙) and choose Preferences from the pop-up menu that appears.
3. Click the Rules button to go to the Rules pane.
4. Click the Add a Rule button.
5. Select an option from the If a Message pop-up menu (such as Is From or Has Subject Containing) and enter an e-mail address or specific text in the field below.
6. To determine what happens to e-mail matching the criteria you just set, select an option from the second pop-up menu.
7. If you chose Move to Folder or Forward To, select a folder or enter an e-mail address. If you chose Move to Trash you don't need to set any more options.
8. Click the Done button.

Stay Connected While Traveling

When traveling or going on vacation, you can keep on the right route by using the GPS features of the iPhone via the included Maps app (see Figure 6-13), via a third-party navigation app, or, for a slightly less high-tech feel, by using the Compass app. You can also control your iPhone in your car using voice recognition.

Another consideration when traveling is to make sure your devices are powered up for the duration of your time away. This can become trickier if you are in a foreign country with different power sockets.

Then there are the questions of how to listen to your music through speakers when you're away from your AirPlay network and how to establish a connection to the Internet to access all your cloud-based content and your iCloud-enabled apps.

Get maps and directions

The Maps app on iOS devices, as well as navigation applications in the App Store, access the location features of your devices to help you navigate. The Apple Maps app can also be controlled by Siri, so you can ask simple questions such as "Where can I get gas?". Siri checks your location and finds nearby gas stations or, if you are already following a set route via the Maps app, finds a place on the way to your destination.

The Maps app can't give you directions by foot or by mass

 transit, so you may want to install the free Google Maps app on your iPhone to get those. At press time, it didn't have an iPad version.

 You might also consider getting the free Waze app for your iPhone or cellular iPad; it's well-liked and provides several features unavailable in Apple's Maps app, including other users' reports of accidents and speed traps, as well as turn-by-turn voice navigation on older iPhones and iPads.

FIGURE 6-13

The Maps app on the iPad

FIGURE 6-14

Turn-by-turn directions in the Maps app on an iPad

Connect to your car's stereo

You can also connect your iOS device to your car's stereo, making it easier to hear the turn-by-turn directions that Siri or your navigation app provides, as well as music from your iPhone or iPad. (Figure 6-14 shows Apple Maps' navigation in action.) These devices typically also let you conduct hands-free calls using your stereo's speakers instead of a Bluetooth headset.

The options depend on the type of stereo system in your car. For just audio playback through your car's speakers, there are cassette adapters (if you still have a cassette player) that connect to your iPhone via a cable. There are also many devices that connect to your iPhone or iPad via Bluetooth and then to your car stereo through an FM radio transmitter. A particularly good one is the $60 GoGroove FlexSmart X2, which has an adjustable microphone that also lets you make calls and issue voice commands to Siri.

Many newer car stereos have Bluetooth and a microphone built in, so they can connect to your iPhone or iPad for audio playback and act as a hands-free mic and speaker for your iPhone. Some stereos also have USB ports that let you connect your iOS device via a cable for audio playback (but not make calls). Some new cars have navigation systems that connect to your iOS device for audio playback, voice control, and phone calls, plus read your e-mails and text messages.

In all these options, how you send your audio is the same: Use the AirPlay controls to select the device as the audio output.

Keep devices charged

Making sure your devices remain charged during a trip is essential if you want to access apps, make calls, use Siri, and have Internet access.

TIP: Set your iOS device to show its battery charge, so you know how much is left with a quick glance at its status bar. Turn on this display in the Settings app's General pane. Tap Usage and then set the Battery Percentage switch to On, as Figure 6-15 shows.

You'll want both a wall charger and a car charger for your iOS devices. There are dozens of such devices available, many for under $15. Compact ones are easier to carry and fit better in tight spaces such as the power ports in some airplanes and airport lobbies. PowerGen, for example, makes inexpensive, compact, and stylish chargers.

Keep in mind that iPads use more power than iPhones and iPods to recharge, so be sure your charger can charge your iPad — many can charge only iPhones and iPods. Look for chargers that output at least 10W or 2.1A on at least one connector; that's what an iPad needs.

Also, be sure to get chargers that have at least two USB ports into which you plug in your iOS devices' USB cables — that way, you can charge two devices at the same time from a single outlet. After all, free outlets can be scarce in hotels and

Turning on the battery percentage display on an iPhone

lobbies, plus many cars have just one cigarette-lighter port in which to plug chargers.

If you travel with a MacBook, consider buying Twelve South's $35 PlugBug, which you piggyback onto your Mac's power brick, so you use only one wall outlet to charge both your Mac and your iOS device.

A convenient option for iPhone users is to use a battery and case combo to give your phone extra power while still keeping it portable. Cases like the $100 Mophie Juice Pack allow you to effectively double the life of your iPhone's battery while keeping it safe from drops and knocks. The Juice Pack allows you to turn on and off charging, too, so you can use the charge from your phone first before charging it with the case's rechargeable battery.

A neat solution when traveling to sunny countries (or at home if you get a lot of sun) is a solar charger for your iOS devices and laptops. By harnessing the sun's rays, you can keep a device running during the day without a plug socket. The $200 PowerMonkey Extreme from Power Traveller is rugged enough to come along with you on any high-octane travels.

If you travel overseas, note that Apple's Mac and iPad charger blocks (but not the iPhone or iPod ones) have detachable plugs, and you can buy the appropriate plugs for other parts of the world from the Apple Store. Otherwise, you might invest in an international travel kit that has the various adapters you might need. Or consider a device like the $20 Insten Universal World Wide Power Adapter that connects to almost any wall socket you might encounter and lets you plug into almost any plug type you may have.

Use portable speakers

AirPlay and Bluetooth speakers (see Chapter 3) aren't simply for your home. With the right speaker, you can listen to music at high quality wherever you happen to be — even if you don't have a power socket. Any battery-powered Bluetooth or AirPlay speaker is an ideal choice (as long as it fits in your bag). You can also opt for a wired speaker that connects directly to your device's headphone socket using a standard mini (3.5mm) connector.

An intriguing type of portable speaker harnesses its surroundings to play sound: You place them on any flat surface and they vibrate that surface to turn it into a speaker. The results differ from surface to surface and location to location but they could be a great option for travelers as they tend to be compact. Such resonance speakers include Lava's $50 Mighty Dwarf.

Another great speaker for the traveling iOS user is the $120 Braven 570.It's not only portable, battery-powered, and able to connect via Bluetooth, but it can also charge your iOS devices while streaming music. You charge its onboard battery pack before you travel, so you have it available as an emergency power supply as well as a convenient way to listen to your music.

Get wireless accessories for travelers

When you're away from your desk, there are things you're bound to miss. A full-size keyboard is one such item for many iPad users. Laptop users may yearn for a separate mouse or touchpad — I know I do. Fortunately, there are ways to re-create the desktop experience while you're on the move.

Wireless keyboards are nothing new, and chances are you already use one with your computer. If so, there's no reason not to take it with you when you're traveling with just your iPhone or iPad — as long as it's a Bluetooth keyboard, of course. Apple's Bluetooth keyboard for the Mac works well with the iPad, too. But Logitech's $70 Tablet Keyboard goes it one better, with special keys for iOS controls such as the Home button and media playback. Plus it comes in a protective case that unfolds into an iPad stand. Zagg's $100 Zaggfolio Case is similar but more stylish.

If you've taken your camera with you on holiday and need to offload images from its memory card so you can carry on shooting, the obvious option is to send the photos to your laptop. But what if you're on an iOS-only trip? One option is to use Apple's $29 iPad Camera Connection Kit for iOS devices that use the old 30-pin Dock connector to transfer photos directly to your device's Camera Roll via an SD Card or direct USB link to the camera. If your iOS device uses the new Lightning connector, Apple sells the $29 USB Camera Adapter and the $29 SD Card Camera Reader separately.

If you want to send photos to the Internet such as to a social network or online photo processor and you don't have a cellular iPad, you can use the Eye-Fi Wi-Fi memory card that connects to your iOS device through the iPad Camera Connection Kit or SD Card Camera Reader to get an Internet connection via a Wi-Fi hotspot. Prices range from $40 to $100 for storage capacities of 4GB to 16GB.

When traveling, you can use Wi-Fi hotspots to connect an iPad to the Internet, and if you travel a lot you may want to invest in a Wi-Fi hotspot service such as Boingo Wireless or, if you're an AT&T broadband customer, take advantage of its

Wi-Fi network whose usage is included in your service. When traveling out of country, you can usually get a prepaid SIM card from a local carrier in the country you're visiting to get local cellular service there. Note that some carriers may not let you use foreign SIMs in your iPhone, so be sure to ask first; there are no such restrictions for iPads.

Alternatively, you could buy a portable wireless hotspot, popularly called a MiFi after a popular brand, that shares a cellular connection with multiple devices simultaneously — iPhones, iPads, computers, and more — over a Wi-Fi signal it generates. Some portable hotspots let you use different SIM cards, making them suited for foreign travel. When buying such a hotspot, note that some require a one- or two-year contract for monthly service, while others allow the use of pay-as-you-go plans.

TIP: When traveling, be sure to disable data roaming on your iOS device so you don't end up paying a premium for use of off-network data. Most carriers let you roam in your home country at no extra charge, but some do not, so be sure to check. When going overseas, turn off the cellular service completely to avoid sky-high international roaming fees — unless you get a local SIM card with prepaid service or purchase an international roaming plan from your carrier. You turn off roaming in the Settings app's General pane: On an iPhone, tap the Cellular label, tap Roaming, then set the Voice Roaming and Data Roaming switches to Off. On an iPad, tap the Cellular Data label in the Settings app, and set the Data Roaming switch to Off if your carrier charges for domestic roaming; unless you have a local SIM for the country you are visiting or an international data plan, always set the International CDMA or International GSM switch to Off. (The options may vary based on your carrier.)

Use an iPhone or iPad as a personal Wi-Fi hotspot

You may not need to buy a personal hotspot — your iPhone or cellular iPad may already be one. The key is whether your carrier allows the device's use as a hotspot, which is also known as tethering. If so, it's easy to set up:

1. Launch the Settings app.
2. Tap the Personal Hotspot label to open the Personal Hotspot pane.
3. Set the Personal Hotspot switch to On (see Figure 6-16).
4. Tap the Wi-Fi Password field and enter a password for the other devices to use to connect.
5. On the other devices, use their standard methods to connect to a Wi-Fi network. The name of your iPhone or iPad should appear in the list of Wi-Fi networks, and those devices should be set to use that iPhone or iPad for Wi-Fi access. The password you set in Step 4 will need to be entered as well.

FIGURE 6-16

Turning the Personal Hotspot service on; here, on an iPhone

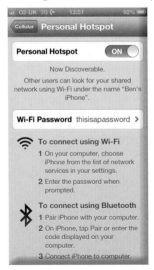

NOTE: Some carriers may charge you extra to enable your iPhone for tethering. Tethering is allowed at no extra charge in pay-as-you-go iPad plans, but some carriers limit you to tethering only when you have an LTE connection active.

NOTE: You cannot use the Personal Hotspot feature to share a Wi-Fi connection with other devices, just a cellular connection. That means you can't set up Wi-Fi access at a hotel or airplane that requires separate access fees per device and share it with others via Personal Hotspot.

7

Staying Organized on the Move

AS WELL AS BEING CONNECTED TO YOUR E-MAIL AND MESSAGES while you're out and about, there are other important considerations to staying organized.

First, there are your calendars. How often do you agree to attend an event only to forget until you are reminded the day before? With a synced calendar in your pocket, you can quickly add an event and even set reminders that appear on all your iCloud-connected devices.

Second, for non-calendar events and ideas, you can use notes and reminders to organize your thoughts so they're ready and waiting on all your devices. You can even use third-party apps to boost your productivity and store a wide range of inspirations as I describe later in this chapter's section on Evernote.

Third, bookmarks can also be synced. Plus, the iCloud Tabs feature automatically lets you access currently and recently open websites on your other iCloud-connected devices, so you can use your iPad at the office to go to a website open at your computer at home — no need to remember its URL.

Fourth, you can even keep important files at your finger tips via iCloud Documents (see Chapter 8) or other cloud storage services like Dropbox. If you are using a Mac remotely, use Back To My Mac to access files on your desktop computer.

Connect Your Calendars

To make the best use of the Calendar app on iOS devices as well as on a Mac (see Figure 7-1) or services like Google Calendar, you first need to set them up to sync with all your devices. Once they are set up, you can edit and view your calendar events on any iCloud device and set alerts to trigger on those devices, too. This is an ideal solution to avoid missing important events, deadlines, and birthdays. As part of the Facebook integration I described in Chapter 6, your Facebook friend's birthdays can also added to your calendar.

FIGURE 7-1

You can access Calendars app on iOS devices, via the web, and (shown here) on a Mac.

You can share your calendars with others to view or share them privately so others can edit them. You can also subscribe to calendars shared by others and access them on all your devices.

Set up Calendars for iCloud

On an iOS device, make sure iCloud is set up correctly and iCloud calendar syncing is turned on (described in Chapter 1) on all the devices whose calendars you want synced. Then, on your iPad, iPhone, or iPod Touch:

1. Launch the Settings app.
2. Tap the iCloud label to open the iCloud pane.
3. Check that the correct iCloud account is listed at the top of the screen and ensure that the Calendars switch is set to On, as Figure 7-2 shows.

FIGURE 7-2

On an iOS device, enable iCloud calendar syncing in the Settings app.

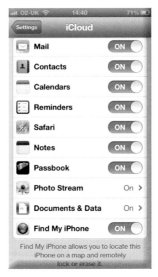

The same principle for setting up Calendars for iCloud on an iOS device applies to iCloud syncing on a Mac: iCloud needs to be running and the calendar syncing feature needs to be turned on. Then, on your Mac.

1. Choose ⇨ System Preferences to open the System Preferences application.
2. Go to the iCloud system preference.
3. Check that the iCloud account you want to use with Calendars is active (see Figure 7-3) and that the Calendars & Reminders option is checked.

PC users can sync calendar entries via iCloud using Microsoft Outlook 2007, 2010, or 2013. Start by installing the iCloud control panel and then turn on syncing. To find out how, head back to Chapter 1. No further steps are needed.

Add other calendar services

You're not limited to iCloud syncing for your calendars. Services like Google Calendar, Hotmail/Outlook.com, and Microsoft Exchange also sync their calendars across devices; most services offer the option to sync calendars at

FIGURE 7-3

Use the iCloud system preferences to turn on iCloud syncing for Calendars on a Mac

regular intervals and, in some cases, use what's called push synchronization to alert you immediately. (Chapter 6 explains how to add a new account.)

On an iOS device, make sure that the calendar service is enabled by following these steps:

1. Launch the Settings app.
2. Tap the Mail, Contacts, Calendars label to open the Mail, Contacts, Calendars pane.
3. Tap the e-mail account linked to the calendar you want to use.
4. Set the Calendars switch to On.

On a Mac:

1. Launch the Calendars app.
2. Choose Calendar ⇨ Preferences and go to the Accounts pane.
3. Click the calendar you want to use in the list at left.
4. In the Account Information subpane that appears, be sure that the Enable This Account option is checked.
5. For services that let you choose how often their calendars are synced, choose the desired interval or, if available, Push in the Refresh Calendars pop-up menu.

Windows users have multiple applications for accessing their calendars, so there's no simple set of steps to follow, but you should look for options that enable the calendar accounts and set the sync frequency.

CHECK THE STATUS OF iCLOUD SERVICES

Every now and again, things don't work the way they should, so you end up fiddling with settings and resetting apps and devices to fix the problem. There's nothing more infuriating than to find that it wasn't your fault at all but that of the service provider.

Apple is no different, so if your e-mail, contacts, notes, or any iCloud syncing features starts going awry, it's worth checking with the iCloud servers before you go into maintenance mode. To do this, visit www.apple.com/support/systemstatus in any browser to see the current condition of several Apple services, including iCloud, iTunes, and Siri. Shown below, this page is one you should bookmark or add to your device's Home screen for quick access.

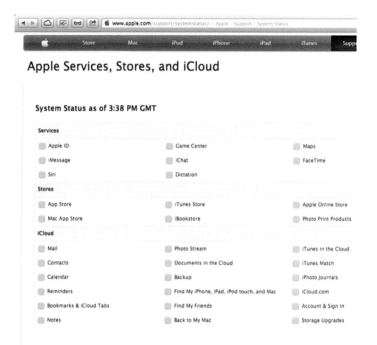

Add a new iCloud calendar

Although you may prefer using one calendar for all your events, you can create multiple calendars that sync between devices. For example, you could create an iCloud calendar for work events and a calendar for home events. When adding a new calendar, you can also choose to show and hide different calendars in the Calendar app, as well as on your Mac. That way, for example, you could have only your work calendar display on your computer so personal appointments are not visible to co-workers but have all your calendars visible on your mobile devices.

To add an iCloud calendar on your iOS device:

1. Launch the Calendars app.
2. Tap the Calendars button to open the Calendars pop-over.
3. Tap the Edit button.
4. Below the list of your iCloud calendars, tap Add Calendar.
5. Enter a name for your calendar and select a calendar color from the list (see Figure 7-4).

FIGURE 7-4

You can create additional calendars for iCloud in the iOS Calendar app (shown here) and Mac's Calendar app.

6. Tap the Done button.

If other calendar services support multiple calendars, they too will have the Add Calendar option in their section of the Calendars pop-over.

To add an iCloud calendar on your Mac:

1. Launch the Calendars app.
2. Choose File ⇨ New Calendar ⇨ iCloud.
3. The Calendars pop-over opens (if it isn't already open), with a new calendar entry labeled "Untitled" in the iCloud section.
4. Enter a name for your calendar; if the calendar name is not pre-selected for editing, double-click it so you can edit it.

If other calendar services support multiple calendars, they will appear in the submenu when you choose File ⇨ New Calendar, and any calendars you create for them appear in their section in the Calendar pop-over.

Now, when you create a new calendar event on any of your devices, you can add it to your new calendar by selecting it from the Calendars pop-over.

Share calendars

You can share your iCloud calendars to keep friends and family informed of your schedule, as well as create a public calendar that anyone can view.

Anyone who has an iCloud account can edit any private calendars you share with them, making this a handy way to organize an event or manage a team.

On an iOS device, to privately share a calendar:

1. Launch the Calendar app.
2. Tap the Calendars button.
3. Tap the Edit button.
4. Tap the name of the calendar you want to share.
5. Tap Add Person under the Shared With section (see Figure 7-5).
6. Enter a name from your contacts or an e-mail address.

FIGURE 7-5

You can share a private calendar with other iCloud users from your iOS device.

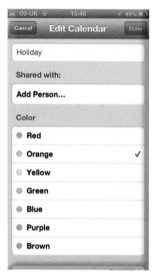

7. Tap the Add button.
8. Tap the name or e-mail address you added under the Shared With section.
9. Set the Allow Editing switch to On or Off as required.

You can continue to add contacts by repeating Steps 5 through 8 until you have invited all the people you want to give access to your calendar. They need to accept the invite before they can view the calendar; you can view the status of each invite from the Edit Calendar screen.

The process for sharing a calendar publicly is similar on an iOS device.

1. Launch the Calendar app.
2. Tap the Calendars button.
3. Tap the Edit button.
4. Tap the name of the Calendar you want to make public.
5. Scroll down and set the Public Calendar switch to On (see Figure 7-6), and wait a minute or so for iCloud to publish the calendar.
6. Tap Share Link when it appears.

FIGURE 7-6

You can share a calendar publicly with other people from your iOS device.

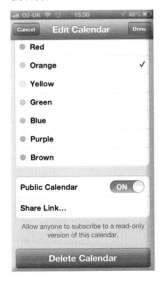

7. In the pop-over that appears, tap Mail to e-mail the link to the public calendar, tap Messages to send it via text message, or tap Copy so you can paste the link into any app you want.

A public calendar can't be edited by others, but it can be viewed by anyone who has its URL. The calendar can be accessed through calendar apps compatible with the iCalendar format, including the Calendar app on iOS devices and Macs and the Outlook app on Windows PCs.

To share a calendar on your Mac:

1. Launch the Calendar app.
2. Click the Calendars button to open the Calendars pop-over.
3. Right-click or Control+click the calendar you want to share.
4. Choose the Sharing Settings option from the menu that appears, or choose Export to export the calendar as a file for sharing.

FIGURE 7-7

Sharing a calendar in the Mac's Calendar app

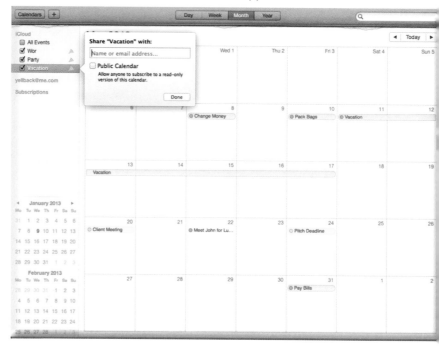

5. Enter one or more e-mail addresses in the Share With field that appears (see Figure 7-7). Separate multiple e-mail addresses or contacts with a comma.
6. To make the calendar public, select the Public option.
7. Click the Done button.

TIP: You can combine public and private sharing for a calendar, so those you share it with via the Add Person button or Share With field can edit the calendar, while everyone else can only read it (using the shared link).

Sync Notes and Reminders

The Notes and Reminders apps on iOS devices and Macs (Figure 7-8 shows the Mac versions) can sync all your notes and reminders to all your iCloud devices. You can also use the Notes and Reminders apps with non-iCloud services such as Gmail for notes and Hotmail for reminders.

FIGURE 7-8

Reminders and Notes sync across your iCloud devices.

For iCloud syncing of notes and reminders to occur on iOS devices, you need to turn on the Notes and Reminders switches in the iCloud pane of the Settings app. On a Mac, be sure that the Notes and Calendars & Reminders options are checked in the iCloud system preference. If you want to sync notes and reminders from a Windows PC running Outlook 2007, 2010, or 2013 to iCloud-connected iOS devices and Macs, go to the iCloud control panel and make sure the Mail, Contacts, Calendars & Tasks option is selected.

Although the Notes app on iOS devices and Macs works in much the same way, there is a difference in the Reminders app you should be aware of: On an iPhone or Mac, you can take advantage of location services to set reminders for when you enter or leave specific locations. This capability is not available for iPads or iPod Touches.

The Notes and Reminders apps work nicely together. Let's say you've written a shopping list in Notes on your Mac and set a reminder to do your shopping that triggers on your iPhone when you are near your local store. After your iPhone alerts you that you need to do your shopping when you are near that store, you can access the shopping list via the Notes app on the iPhone — the note you entered on the Mac is synced to the iPhone via iCloud.

Create reminders

On an iOS device, creating a reminder is as easy as setting a date and time or, if you simply want to add a to-do item to your list, entering text to be stored across all your devices.

1. Launch the Reminders app.
2. Tap the desired list in the iCloud section (Reminders is the default, but you can add more using the Create New List option).
3. Tap on any blank area in the list below any existing reminders.
4. Type your reminder.
5. On an iPhone or iPod Touch, tap the More button (the > icon) that appears to the right of your reminder text to open the Details screen. On an iPad, tap outside your new reminder, then tap the new reminder itself to open the Details pop-over.

FIGURE 7-9

Your iPhone (shown here) or Mac can remind you when you arrive at or leave a specified location.

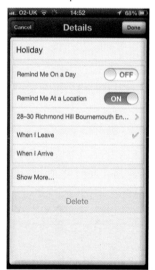

6. To be reminded with an alert on a day or location, set the relevant switch — Remind Me on a Day and/or At a Location — to the On position and add information to the fields that appear (see Figure 7-9).

    ○ For a date, tap the field showing the current date and time to change it to a different date and time. Tap repeat to set up a repeating reminder; the options are None, Every Day, Every Week, Every 2 Weeks, Every Month, and Every Year.

    ○ For a location (available only on the iPhone and the Mac), the current location appears; tap it to change it to an address of your choice. Tap either When I Leave or When I Arrive to set what behavior triggers the reminder.

7. If you want to set the priority level of a reminder, tap the Priority option, then choose from None, Low, Medium, and High, as Figure 7-10 shows. If you don't see the Priority option, tap Show More.

8. If you have multiple reminder lists set up, tap the List option to assign which list the reminder is placed in. Again, if you don't see the List option, tap Show

FIGURE 7-10

You can edit the priority level of a reminder and add notes (here, shown on a Mac)

More. (If you have only one list, this option does not display.)

9. Tap the Done button.

The Reminders app on a Mac works similarly. But in Step 5 above, the *i* icon appear when you tap the reminder; tap the *i* icon to open the Details pop-over.

You can create reminders on a PC using Outlook's tasks feature; if you've enable iCloud syncing, these tasks will sync with Reminders on your iOS devices and Mac.

You can also access reminders via the iCloud.com website from most devices and computers. After signing in with your iCloud account and password, click the Reminders button to open the Reminders app.

Create reminders with Siri on an iOS device

Apple's Siri service (available on the iPhone 4S and 5 and on the third-generation iPad, fourth-generation iPad, and iPad Mini when connected to the Internet) offers the quickest route to creating a reminder when using an iOS device. Simply tap and hold the device's Home button, wait for the Siri chime, and speak a command starting with the words "Remind me." The command could be as simple as "Remind me to call James" (see Figure 7-11) or complex, including locations or times, such as "Remind me to pick up milk when I leave work" or "Remind me to pick up my dry cleaning at four PM."

As well as creating reminders, you can use Siri to set alarms and timers using the iOS Clock app on compatible devices. Use commands like "Set a timer for five minutes" or "Wake me up at three," to have Siri set alarms for the specified time or set a countdown timer to alert you when a specific time has elapsed.

I find the voice-initiated reminders and timers on my iPhone to be invaluable when cooking because I always carry my phone and can hear the alarm wherever I am. It's much

FIGURE 7-11

Siri understands when to set a reminder and often asks for additional information

more reliable than the kitchen timer that I can't really hear when I leave the kitchen and then get distracted, which often results in a much louder alarm — my fire alarm — blaring when whatever's in the oven or on the stove begins to smoke.

Create reminder lists

If you are working on multiple projects or you don't want to mix your work and home reminders, you can group reminders into separate lists. Once you have created a list, you can quickly jump between groups in the Reminders app to see specific sets of reminders. You can also use the calendar view to show all the reminders for a specific day.

To create a list on an iPad, just tap the Create New List option under the desired service (such as iCloud), then enter your preferred name for that list.

On an iPhone or iPod Touch, tap the Lists button (≡) to open the Lists screen, then tap the Create New List option under the desired service (such as iCloud), enter your preferred name for that list, and tap Done.

On a Mac, tap the Add button (the + icon), then enter your preferred name. If you have multiple reminder accounts set up, a pop-up menu appears when you tap the Add button, letting you select the service to add the list to, such as iCloud.

On iCloud.com in your browser, sign in and then open the Reminders app. Tap the Add button (the + icon), then enter your preferred name. This list is added to your iCloud account.

On a Mac or Windows PC, use the calendar-creation feature in your version of Outlook. This list is added to your Exchange account.

Share reminder lists

Sharing a list of reminders allows you to delegate tasks to others who have iCloud accounts — ideal for planning events or collaborating on projects. Unfortunately, you can only share reminder lists from iCloud.com and the Mac version of Reminders, not from iOS devices. When someone accepts the invitation to a shared list, he or she can see all the reminders in that list, mark them as completed, and add new reminders to it.

1. Launch the Mac Reminders app or visit iCloud.com and access the Web-based Reminders app.
2. Hover your cursor over the list you want to share until the Share button (📶) appears.
3. Click the Share button (📶).
4. Enter the contact names or e-mail addresses you want to share the list with in the provided field, separating each name with a comma (see Figure 7-12).
5. Click the Done button.

FIGURE 7-12

You can share a Reminders list with other iCloud users from the Mac or iCloud.com

Set the default reminders list and sync frequency

If you have several reminders lists, one is the default that all new reminders are assumed to belong to unless you specify a different list. So how do you specify what the default list is?

On an iOS device, you set the default reminders list in the Settings app. Go to the Reminders pane, tap the Default List section, and then tap the name of the list you want to use most often. In this pane, you also can set how far back you want your reminders to sync, starting with reminders created two weeks ago to the beginning of time (All Reminders).

On a Mac, you can't set the default reminders list. So be sure to select the desired list first in the app before creating a new reminder. You also can't set how far back to sync reminders; all reminders are synced so your Mac has the full set forever.

Create and Share Notes

You can use the Notes app to created synced notes on iOS devices, Macs, and on any device via the iCloud.com website,

FIGURE 7-13

The first line of text in a note is also used as the note title

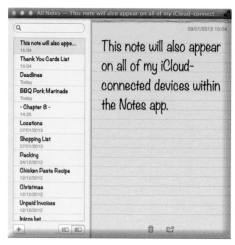

as well as sync notes created on third-party e-mail services if linked to the Notes app. Notes are simple text documents that remain in sync on all your iCloud devices and include options for formatting and adding attachments.

1. Launch the Notes app on an iOS device, via the iCloud.com website, or on a Mac.
2. Click the Add button (the + icon) to create a new note; on the Mac, you can also press ⌘+N.
3. Tap the main note area and type your note's text (see Figure 7-13).

Apply formatting and add attachments to notes

When using the Notes app on a Mac or via the iCloud.com website, you can apply basic formatting and text transformations as well as add file attachments to a note. Some formatting changes are visible on all devices but attachments are not displayed on iOS devices, appearing instead as a paperclip to denote an attachment (see Figure 7-14).

FIGURE 7-14

If a paperclip icon appears on a note on your iOS device, the note has an attachment that can't be displayed.

The Mac version of the Notes app offers options for editing and adding attachments and so is ideal for creating a note for syncing with other devices.

1. Launch the Notes app.
2. Select an existing note or create a new note.
3. Select a section of text and press ⌘+T to access the Fonts pane (see Figure 7-15).
4. Edit your text.
5. To add an attachment, drag and drop a file onto the note. Some attachments, such as images, will appear in the body of the note while others will appear as a paperclip icon.

The iCloud.com Notes app offers more formatting and attachment options than Notes on iOS devices but fewer options than the Mac version of the Notes app.

1. Log in to your iCloud account at iCloud.com and click the Notes button to open the Notes app.
2. Create a new note or access an existing note.

FIGURE 7-15

You can adjust a note's font and other formatting when editing it on a Mac.

3. Select the text you want to format and right-click or Control+click in the selection to open a contextual menu.

4. Use the contextual menu options to format the text. You can adjust the font by choosing Transformations ⇨ Font (see Figure 7-16) and adjust the paragraph formatting by choosing Transformations ⇨ Paragraph Direction.

5. To add an attachment, copy its content — for example, from Preview for an image or Acrobat for a PDF document — and right-click or Control+click the note to display a contextual menu. From that menu, choose Paste. You can also click on the note and press ⌘+V to paste the copied content.

Change the default notes font

You can set a default font for the Notes app on each of your devices. (You set them separately; the default font in one does not change the default font another.) On a Mac, choose Format ⇨ Font ⇨ Default Font and then tap the desired font

FIGURE 7-16

Adjusting a note's fonts in the iCloud.com Notes app

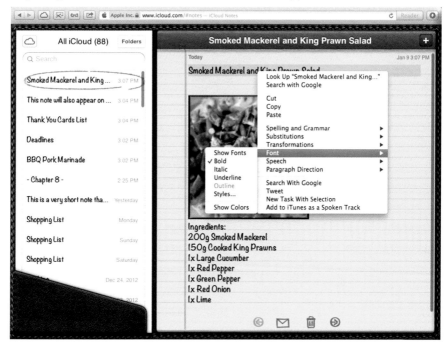

in the list there. Either way, your choices are Noteworthy, Helvetica, and Marker Felt. (You can't set the default font for the iCloud.com Notes app.)

Create notes folders

By default, the Notes app creates folders of notes for each note location. On a Mac, the Notes app creates the On My Mac folder as well as an iCloud folder and a folder for any other services using Notes, such as Gmail. You can create your own folders in the Notes app on a Mac and access them from all your iCloud-connected devices:

1. Launch the Notes app.
2. If the folders list (see the left side of Figure 7-17) isn't visible, choose View ⇨ Show Folders List to display it.
3. Right-click or Control+click the folders list.
4. Choose New Folder from the contextual menu that appears.

FIGURE 7-17

Folders help you to organize groups of notes.

5. Type a name for your folder in the field that appears.
6. To add notes to your new folder, select that folder in the folders list and create a note the usual way.

Share notes

You can share notes from the Notes app on any of your devices by tapping or clicking the Share button (⤴). Depending on the device used, the options in the menu or pop-over that appears include sending the note as an e-mail, sending it as a text message, copying its content, and printing it.

Of course, you can also copy content from the note and then paste it into e-mails, text messages, documents, and anything else that can accept pasted text.

Use non-iCloud notes with the Notes app

Some e-mail services, such as Gmail and many IMAP-based e-mail services, allow you to sync with the Notes app on all your devices. Once you have a non-iCloud e-mail account on any of your devices, go to the Mail, Contacts, Calendars

FIGURE 7-18

Some third-party e-mail services such as Gmail can also sync with the Notes app.

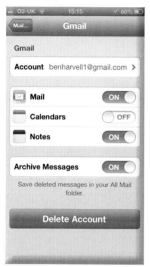

pane in the Settings app in iOS (see Figure 7-18) device or go to the Mail, Contacts, Calendars system preference on a Mac to check whether your account supports notes: Tap or click the name of the service to see if the Notes option appears for it. If so, you can sync to the Notes app by setting the Notes switch to On.

Set the default Notes account

If you are using more than one account with the Notes app — iCloud and Gmail for example — you can set the default account for Notes app. On a Mac, choose Notes ⇨ Default Account, then choose the account you want to be the default. On an iOS device, go to the Settings app's Notes pane and tap the Default Account field to select the account you want to use as the default. (At iCloud.com, you can work only with your iCloud account's notes, so there's no option to set a default account.)

Dictate Text

On compatible iOS devices, you'll see the Dictate button (🎤) next to the space bar in most apps that use the onscreen keyboard. It's a surprisingly powerful feature: You can speak to your device rather than type. You do need to be connected to the Internet for this feature to work, so your iOS device can tap into Apple's speech-to-text servers and provide the fairly accurate translation even for long blocks of spoken text.

Dictation works with Siri, so you can even tell Siri to "take a note" and then speak your note for Apple's servers to transcribe into the active text field, as Figure 7-19 shows.

If you don't see the Dictate button (🎤), go to the Settings app's General pane in your iOS device and then tap the Siri label to open the Siri pane. Make sure the Siri switch is set to On to enable dictation (and Siri). If you don't have the Siri label, your iOS device can't do dictation.

OS X Mountain Lion also supports dictation in most apps, if you have a recent-model Mac. By default, you press the Fn key twice to turn on dictation; you can change this key in the

FIGURE 7-19

Siri can transcribe notes you dictate on your iOS device.

Dictation & Speech system preference, which is also where you turn dictation on or off.

When dictating, you use common punctuation such as commas, periods, new paragraphs, new lines, question marks, and exclamation points by simply saying their names aloud, although inflection is important to ensure that the word "comma" doesn't appear where you wanted to insert a comma itself (,) as a break in the text.

For quick notes and ideas, the built-in dictation is an easy way to get your thoughts transcribed. But, if you're after more powerful speech recognition, you should look at third-party apps for iOS and OS X.

I recommend you try the free Dragon Dictation by Nuance Communications. It's does an impressive job of understanding and transcribing what you speak — and is fast. In addition to dictating in a text field, Dragon Dictation allows you to submit voice controlled tweets to Twitter (see Figure 7-20) and updates to Facebook. Like Apple's own dictation service, you do need an active Internet connection so Dragon Dictation can access Nuance's speech-to-text servers. A full-blown

FIGURE 7-20

Dragon Dictation allows you to update Twitter using only your voice.

TRANSLATE FOREIGN LANGUAGES

When you're in a foreign country, an iOS device can be indispensable for conversing with locals and understanding signs and directions. Two of the most incredible, almost magic apps I've come across can help in this situation.

The first is called iTranslate Voice, shown at right. Available for $0.99, Sonico's iTranslate Voice and iTranslate Voice HD for iPad listens to what you say and translates it to a foreign language in both text and audio forms. Not only is this handy when trying the right phrasing abroad, it's also a great learning tool to help you perfect your pronunciation and pick up vocabulary. A range of languages are available including Spanish, French, Italian, and Portuguese and you can switch the translation direction at any time to help you understand what you're saying or what you're being asked.

The second magical language app I've used on a regular basis is Word Lens by Quest Visual, an app that has to be seen to be believed. Simply hold your iPhone up to a sign, menu, or any text written in a supported language and the text is translated into English. The app even tries to retain the

version of this software called Dragon Naturally Speaking is available for Mac and PC; it not only supports dictation but also lets you control your computer with voice commands. The software learns the way you speak too, so even you mumblers or gabblers should see great results over time.

Surf the Web More Easily with Bookmarks

Bookmarks are hardly a new phenomenon, so I'm amazed when people tell me they don't use them. Bookmarking a website is a quick way to revisit a website on your computer, without having to remember or type in the cryptic URLs. The mobile revolution now lets you carry those easy-access

original font for complete clarity. Language packs for French, Spanish, English, and Italian cost $4.99 each.

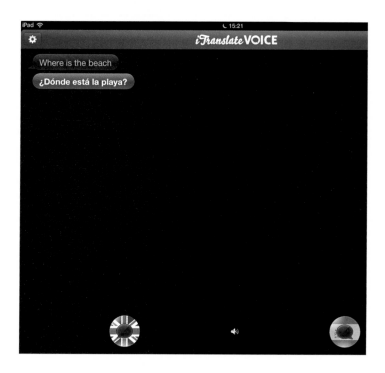

shortcuts wherever you go. Even better, thanks to iCloud, if you make a change to a bookmark or add a new one, it'll appear on all your iCloud devices.

With iCloud, bookmarks take on new forms with great tools like Reading List and iCloud Tabs. Reading List lets you bookmark links to be read later, then deletes them once you've gone to the web page, so your bookmarks don't get cluttered with links that were only meant to be temporary reminders. iCloud Tabs shows you the web pages currently and recently open on other iOS devices and Macs, so you can pick up where you left off as you change devices.

Get your bookmarks in order

If you already have bookmarks saved on one of your devices, you're already part of the way to syncing them. If not, you can start with an empty set of bookmarks. Either way, I strongly recommend you do the heavy bookmark lifting on your computer (in Safari on a Mac or your choice of Safari or Internet Explorer on a Windows PC). What you want to do is create your bookmarks on that computer (or clean up the ones it already has), so it serves as the initial master bookmarks list for when you later sync other devices' bookmarks with it. Yes, you can do this work on your iOS device, but you'll find it is easier to do on a computer.

If you have bookmarks stored in another browser, first import them into Safari on your computer to help put together that master bookmark list. All browsers differ, but the export option is normally in the bookmark. In Safari on your computer, choose File ➪ Import Bookmarks, select the exported bookmarks file, and click the Import button to add them to Safari.

Now it's time to tidy up your bookmarks. In Safari, choose Bookmarks ➪ Show All Bookmarks to see all your bookmarks. The process in Windows' Internet Explorer varies based on the version of IE you use, but look for a similar setting. On an iOS device, tap the Bookmarks button (📖) in Safari to open the Bookmarks screen or pop-over.

Delete unwanted bookmarks, add missing bookmarks, create new folders, and organize bookmarks in folders. On an iOS device, tap the Edit button to get these controls. On a computer, simply select, delete, and drag and drop links as you want, and use the Bookmarks menu for other operations.

When Safari (or Internet Explorer) are set up with your master bookmarks, make sure that Safari is selected in the iCloud system preference on the Mac or that Browser is selected in the iCloud control panel in Windows (click Options to select whether Safari or Internet Explorer is synced; you can't sync both). Then, on each iOS device, go to the Settings app's iCloud pane and make sure the Safari switch is set to On. Your devices will sync their bookmarks (give it up to an hour the first time).

REMEMBER: The devices need an active Internet connection to sync.

After the devices all sync up their bookmarks, you may find some duplicates because of bookmarks that may have been on your iOS devices or other computers connected to your iCloud account. Go to any computer or iOS device to clean up the bookmarks, and in a short time you'll see the other devices cleaned themselves up as well after they've synced.

The hard-core approach to cleaning up your bookmarks is to disable iCloud syncing on all your devices, then delete all their bookmarks — except for the computer or device that has your master bookmark list. Once that master is cleaned up, turn on bookmark syncing on all your devices so the cleaned-up bookmarks sync to the other devices.

Add bookmarks individually

To add bookmarks as you come across pages you want to save the links to, just tap or click the Share button ( ) in Safari. When you add a bookmark, you get the option to store it in a bookmarks folder, in the bookmarks bar (at the top of the screen in Safari on a computer or iPad), or in your general bookmarks.

Edit the bookmarks bar

The Safari bookmarks bar on a computer or iPad is the easiest route to accessing your commonly used bookmarks because they are always available. To display the bookmarks bar in Safari on a computer, choose View ⇨ Show Bookmarks. On an iPad, go to the Settings app's Safari pane and set the Always Show Bookmarks Bar switch to On. The bookmarks bar displays a list of bookmarks or bookmark folders above the page you are viewing, below the URL bar.

TIP: On an iPhone or iPod Touch, the bookmarks bar is simply a folder in the Bookmarks screen, so it doesn't have that always-visible convenience as on the iPad or a computer. But it does sync with those devices, so you can use it to add bookmarks that will sync to the bookmarks bar on the iPad and computer.

As you would expect from Apple, the bookmarks bar is also synced between devices when using iCloud syncing so you have access to the same bookmarks on all your devices.

Add bookmarks to your iOS device's Home screen

For your most important bookmarks, web apps, or websites, you can add a bookmark to your iOS device's Home screen that looks like an app icon, so you can tap it to open that web page as if it were an app.

iOS grabs the web page's icon (if its developers gave it one) or takes a snapshot of the current screen (if not) for use as that app icon. That app icon can be put in folders, deleted, and moved just like any app icon.

The process to create a bookmark icon on the Home screen is simple:

1. Launch the Safari browser.
2. In the Safari URL bar, enter the URL of the web page you want to visit.
3. When the page has loaded, tap the Share button (↪).
4. Tap the Add to Home Screen button.
5. Enter a name for the bookmark's icon using the onscreen keyboard.
6. Tap the Add button. The icon is added to your device's Home screen.

Sync bookmarks from different browsers to iCloud

I won't tell anyone if you admit that you use another browser in addition to Safari. The truth is, many people use browsers such as Firefox or Chrome based on their personal preference. But when you use more than one browser, it becomes hard to keep your bookmarks in sync: Which browser has which bookmarks?

And iCloud bookmark syncing only syncs the bookmarks stored in Safari (or Internet Explorer on a Windows PC, if you set it to do so).

Fortunately, there is a way to sync your bookmarks across the major browsers: Xmarks Bookmark Sync (www.xmarks. com). It syncs bookmarks in Firefox (in Windows, OS X, and Linux), Safari (in OS X only), Internet Explorer (a Windows-only browser), and Chrome (in Windows, OS X, and Linux). You sign up for an account and then install the free Xmarks

STAY STEALTHY WITH PRIVATE BROWSING

Like most browsers, Safari has a feature that prevents any information about the sites you visit being recorded. It's called Private Browsing, and it keeps your entire browser session private by not recording your history of pages visited, by blocking all cookies that websites may use to track your presence (and remember previous visits), and by disabling the syncing of iCloud Tabs with other devices. Private Browsing is perfect for when you're doing your holiday shopping or planning a surprise on a shared device or a device that isn't yours.

On the computer version of Safari, you enable Private Browsing by choosing Safari ⇨ Private Browsing on the Mac or ✿ ⇨ Private Browsing in Windows. The "Private" label appears in the URL bar; click it to turn off Private Browsing.

On an iOS device, you enable Private Browsing in the Settings app's Privacy pane: Set the Private Browsing Switch to On. In Safari, the normally blue and light gray menu bars turn to black and dark gray as a reminder. Go back to the Privacy pane to turn off Private Browsing; the standard Safari color scheme returns.

plug-in for each browser you have, on each computer you have. The Xmarks service then syncs the bookmarks across the browsers — just keep in mind that its not as fast as iCloud is, so be patient. Then, iCloud will sync the bookmarks from Safari on your Mac or Internet Explorer on your PC to your iOS devices. Or you can buy the $12 annual service, which adds support for various mobile devices (including iOS) and an iCloud Tabs-like capability. The only issue with Xmarks is that it does not work with Safari for Windows, so if that's the browser you sync to iOS devices with, you're out of luck.

Create a Reading List for access anywhere on any device

iCloud's Safari syncing also syncs your Reading List bookmarks. The Reading List holds the links you tagged to read later. With iCloud, you can read them on any connected devices. Even better, Reading List stores full web pages so, even if you don't have an Internet connection, you can view the page. Once you've read a page stored in the Reading List, it is removed, so you only see bookmarks to what you haven't yet read. (Use regular bookmarks instead for links you want to return to time and again.)

You access the Reading List by clicking the Reading List button (⊖⊖) in Safari on a computer and from the Bookmarks screen or pop-over on an iOS device. On an iPad's Bookmarks pop-over, tap the Reading List button (⊖⊖) at the bottom of the pop-over to see a list of your Reading List bookmarks. On an iPhone or iPod Touch, tap the Reading List folder at the top of the Bookmarks screen to see the list of saved items.

NOTE: When you're using a cellular connection to access the Internet, such as from your iPhone, the Reading List may not synchronize. If not, cellular syncing is probably disabled on your device to reduce your data usage. You can turn it on in the Settings app's Safari pane via the Use Cellular Data switch.

To add a link to the Reading List, click or tap the Share button (📤) in Safari, then choose Add to Reading List from the menu (on a computer) or pop-over (on an iOS device) that appears.

Access open tabs in Safari on any device with iCloud Tabs

iCloud Tabs (see Figure 7-21) is a simple and incredibly handy feature. Click the iCloud Tabs button (☁) in Safari on a computer or the iPad to get a list of currently and recently open web pages on your other iOS devices. On an iPhone or iPod Touch, tap the Bookmarks button (📖) and then tap iCloud Tabs in the screen that appears to see that list.

iCloud Tabs lets you start reading a website on one device and finish reading on another. Or easily go back to a website open on a different device, such as to open a web page you were reading at home this morning later in the day from work.

FIGURE 7-21

iCloud Tabs in Safari on an iPhone

Quickly store all open tabs as bookmarks in Safari

The computer version of Safari offers a quick way to store all open pages (browser tabs) as a set of bookmarks. That's really handy such as when you are researching a topic across multiple websites or comparing products online. When you save a group of tabs as bookmarks, Safari automatically creates a folder for them. Here's the process:

1. Launch Safari.
2. Open all the web pages you want to save. Make sure each page is in its own tab, not in separate windows.
3. Choose Bookmarks ⇨ Add Bookmarks for These Tabs.
4. In the pop-over that appears, select the location where you would like to store the folder of tab bookmarks.
5. Enter a name for the folder that will contain the tabs (see Figure 7-22).
6. Click the Add button.

TIP: When reading web pages on the smaller screen of an iPhone or iPod Touch, you can put the browser in full-screen mode — if you're running iOS 6, that is. Simply rotate the device to landscape orientation and tap the Full Screen button (⤢) at the bottom right of the screen. Tap it again to get back the menu bar and status bar. Safari on the Mac also has a full-screen mode: Tap the Full Screen button (⤢) at the upper right of the window or choose View ⇨ Enter Full Screen. (When in full-screen mode on the Mac, hover the pointer at the top of the screen until the menu bar appears, then click the Full Screen button to revert to normal view.)

FIGURE 7-22

Creating bookmarks from tabs in Safari for better browsing

Organize Yourself with Evernote

For a completely different but useful way to store just about anything digital across your devices, Evernote is the answer. Part organizer, part bookmark tool, part gallery, part to-do list, the

A Day in the Life: Calendars, Notes, Reminders, and Bookmarks

A national holiday is coming up and you're heading home to see your family. While planning your trip, you create a calendar to help plot your movements over the long weekend. As many family members are attending, you send each one an invitation to share the calendar. Each accepts the invitation and adds his or her own itineraries so everyone can keep track of where everyone will be and when.

As you prepare to travel, you create a list of things you need to do in the Reminders app. Some tasks will be up to you, while others can be delegated to other members of the family, so you share the list you created. As everyone completes their respective tasks, they check off the tasks on the list. When the time comes to depart, everyone receives a reminder on his or her iPhone or iPad that it's time to go.

On the journey home, you think of a couple of stories you want to share with the family later, so you type them into the Notes app to jog your memory when you get home. (You're not driving, obviously!) You then realize that you could pass the time by finishing reading a blog post you started that morning before you left for the long weekend, but you can't remember the web address. Tapping the iCloud Tabs button (☁) on your cellular-connected iPad, you find the page that was open on your computer at home and finish reading the post. When you're done, you make sure to bookmark the site so you can view future posts.

app is an all-in-one solution for projects — or for simply gathering information that interests you.

Whether you're planning a trip, researching a project, or anything else, you can keep all the associated data in one place with Evernote, including images, text, links, and PDF files. The app can even turn printed or handwritten notes you add into searchable text, so you don't miss important documents and information when searching in a project. Notebooks created in Evernote can be shared with and used to collaborate on projects. It's a great next step after using Apple's Notes app, for more flexible information management.

Evernote syncs among Macs, PCs, and iOS devices, and it has a web interface so you can guarantee that all the information you store is kept safe. The app and service are free. Evernote offers a $45 annual subscription option that unlocks advanced features. But beginners should be happy with the basic, free features — at least for a while.

8

Back Up, Store, and Share Files

ALTHOUGH BACKUP AND ONLINE STORAGE MIGHT NOT HAVE THE same appeal as streaming movies, games, and photos, the same omnipresent iCloud connection they rely on among all your devices can make a real difference to how you work and keep organized. It also makes life a lot easier when performing basic functions like printing and sharing files among computers or with friends and family.

Back Up via iCloud

iCloud backup is available for any iOS device running iOS 5 or later with an iCloud account. With iCloud backup enabled, your device will automatically back up important information to the iCloud servers each day, and you can restore your device from that backup at any time. It also means that, should you replace your current device, you can restore the new device using the iCloud backup. This, of course, negates the requirement for your device to ever have to be connected directly to a computer to use iTunes for backup.

You can use either iCloud backup or the traditional iTunes backup method — but not both — to automatically back up your important information, such as your camera roll in the Photos App, your account settings, the contents of your apps, and iCloud documents. All your iTunes Store purchases, including books, movies, music, TV shows, and apps, are backed up, with an infinite amount of space available for them. Both iCloud backup and iTunes backup save all those files, but only iTunes backup saves media files that you didn't buy through the iTunes Store.

You can turn iCloud backup on directly from the device you want to use it with, as Figure 8-1 shows, or select iCloud backup in iTunes for your device, as Figure 8-2 shows. iCloud backup runs when your device is locked, has a Wi-Fi Internet connection, and is connected to a power source. You can manually start a backup to iCloud by going to the Settings

FIGURE 8-1

Turning on iCloud backup on an iOS device

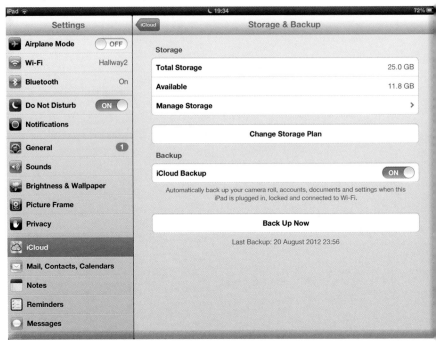

app's iCloud pane, tapping Storage & Backup, and then tapping Back Up Now.

Even if you use iCloud backup, you can still manually back up to your computer.

Manually back up to iTunes

Even if you have iCloud Backup turned on, you can still manually back up your device to your computer using iTunes to have a backup available on your computer.

From iTunes on your computer:

1. Either connect your iOS device via a USB cable to your computer or ensure that the device is on the same network as your computer.

2. Your device's name will appear on a button at the top right of the window, next to the Store button. Click your device's name to continue. If you have multiple iOS devices, the Devices button appears instead; click

FIGURE 8-2

FIGURE 8-2

Turning on iCloud backup in iTunes on your computer

it to open a pop-over listing your devices, then choose the one you want to back up.

3. A screen with your device's information and storage capacity is shown. Click the Back Up Now button to begin the backup.

4. Click the Done button when finished.

TIP: If you click Sync instead of Back Up Now, you'll still back up your iOS device to iTunes. But you'll also transfer anything new in iTunes on your computer to that iOS device.

From your iOS device:

1. Make sure that your iOS device is connected to the same network as your computer and iTunes is running on that computer.

2. Launch the Settings app.

3. Go to the General pane.

4. Tap iTunes Wi-Fi Sync.

5. Tap Sync Now; if the option is grayed out, that means your iOS device and/or computer are not on the right network or that iTunes is not running on your computer.

Manage iCloud storage

Every iCloud user gets 5GB of free storage in iCloud, shared across all their devices. That 5GB limit does not include content you purchased from the iTunes Store nor the first 10,000 photos saved in your Photo Stream. The rest of your iCloud backups, as well as iCloud e-mail messages, apps' contents, and documents synced via iCloud Documents do count against that limit.

You can buy more iCloud storage from your iOS device: Go to the iCloud pane in the Settings app, tap Storage & Backup, tap Change Storage Plan, and choose how much storage you want. Currently, Apple charges $20 per year for an extra 10GB (so you get 15GB altogether), $40 for an additional 20GB, and $100 for an additional 50GB. Each year, Apple will charge your iCloud storage plan's cost from your iTunes Store account, until you change the storage amount.

As Figure 8-3 shows, you can see how much storage you've used in iCloud. In the Settings app's iCloud pane, tap Storage & Backup, and then tap Manage Storage. In the Manage Storage pane that appears, you'll see a list of iOS devices' backups as well as the amount of data used by various apps on your current iOS device and used by your iCloud e-mail account. Tap an iOS device's name to open the Info pane that displays the backup storage used by that device.

From the Manage Storage pane, you see how much data each app uses on the current OS device. But the real action occurs in the Info pane. Tap a device's name in the Backups list to open the Info pane and see how much iCloud storage it is using and when it was last backed up.

FIGURE 8-3

You can monitor your iCloud storage usage from your iOS device's Settings app.

You can also delete backups of any iOS devices associated to your iCloud account, such as when you give your old iPad to your kid. In the Info pane, tap Delete Backup to delete the backup in iCloud (the device is not wiped, just its iCloud backup).

For your current device only (if it's backed up to iCloud), the Info pane also shows a list of apps in the Backup Options section, as Figure 8-4 shows. Use the switches to the right of each app to determine whether its contents are backed up; if an app's switch is set to On, its contents are backed up to iCloud.

Restore devices from iCloud backups

You can use the backups stored in iCloud in one of two ways.

FIGURE 8-4

You can specify which apps' contents are saved to iCloud backup.

> ◉ If you are setting up a device for the first time, you are asked if you want to restore from an iCloud backup as part of the device setup. This option is possible only if you have entered your Apple ID and are connected to the Internet via a Wi-Fi network, whether you are setting up the device on the device itself or via iTunes on your computer.
>
> ◉ If your iOS device is not working properly, you can connect it via USB cable (not Wi-Fi) to your computer and in iTunes select a backup to restore it from, bringing the device back to that previous state. After selecting your iOS device from the Devices button, click Restore Backup in the Summary pane that appears. (This technique works with backups stored in iCloud or on your computer.)

TIP: If your device doesn't appear in iTunes when you want to restore it, you may need to put it in recovery mode or

Device Firmware Update (DFU) mode. After ensuring that the iOS device is connected to your computer via a USB cable and iTunes is running, hold the Sleep/Wake button and Home button on the device at the same time. When the screen goes blank, release the Sleep/Wake button while continuing to hold the Home button until iTunes recognizes the device.

Buy more iCloud storage

If you are running low on iCloud storage, you can increase your storage plan by buying a larger amount of storage using iCloud Control Panel on a Windows PC and the iCloud section of System Preferences on a Mac. To increase your storage allowance on an iOS device, follow these steps:

1. Launch the Settings app.
2. Tap iCloud.
3. Tap Storage & Backup.
4. Tap Change Storage Plan.
5. Tap the amount of storage you would like to buy.
6. Tap the Buy button (see Figure 8-5).

FIGURE 8-5

Purchasing additional iCloud storage

BACK UP YOUR MAC, TOO

Apple makes it really easy to back up your iOS device; if the iOS device is plugged in and connected to the Internet via a Wi-Fi network, it will back up once a day automatically to iCloud or — if your computer is running, connected to the same network as the iOS device, and iTunes is running — to your computer, depending on whether you selected iCloud backup or iTunes backup.

But what about your Mac? Apple makes backup easy on a Mac as well, if you connect an external hard drive to it via a cable or a network connection. OS X comes with a utility called Time Machine that regularly backs up your Mac, even as you work, so you can restore a Mac's files from it — including your iTunes backups — or move the Mac's contents to a new Mac. Once you've turned on Time Machine, you can just let it do its thing.

And setting up is easy:

1. Choose ➪ System Preferences and click Time Machine to open the Time Machine system preference.

2. Click Select Disk and then choose the backup disk to use from the settings sheet that appears.

3. If you don't want to back up all the disks connected to your Mac or you want to exclude specific folders, click the Options button, then click the Add button (the + icon) to select what you don't want backed up. Repeat this action for

Use iCloud.com

iCloud.com is where you can find web versions of the Mail, Contacts, Calendar, Notes, Reminders, and Find My iPhone apps, as well as iCloud documents stored by Apple's iWork apps (Pages, Keynote, and Numbers).

You can sign into iCloud.com from any computer with an Internet connection using your Apple ID and password (see Figure 8-6) and work in almost the same way as you would on your computer or iOS device. Signing in remotely can be handy when traveling without your computer or iOS devices,

each item to exclude, then click Save.

4. Set the Time Machine switch to On.

5. Close the Time Machine system preference. Your Mac will now keep itself backed up without your intervention (the first time may take a few hours).

You can restore individual files by launching the Time Machine app from your Mac's Applications folder, then choosing which file from which date to restore. Or you can restore an entire Mac from a Time Machine backup, using the Disk Utility application or when running Disk Recovery mode. For more details, I recommend you pick up a book on OS X, such as Wiley's *OS X Mountain Lion Bible*.

If you use Windows, you'll need backup software; it's not part of Windows.

allowing you to access all your information wherever you happen to be.

TIP: You also have the option to remain signed in on the computer you are currently using by checking the box below the sign-in box. This isn't advisable unless you're using a secure computer, as it allows others using the computer to access your iCloud account later.

Once you've signed into iCloud.com, the home screen appears with icons for each app. Click an app's icon to open it. When in an app, click the iCloud button (⌂) at upper left to return to the home screen.

FIGURE 8-6

Signing in to iCloud.com

Edit iCloud settings online

The Mail, Contacts, and Calendar apps available on iCloud.com have their own settings that can be edited by clicking the Settings button (⚙) that appears in the upper right of the app screen.

You can also adjust general settings for your iCloud account by clicking your name at the top right of the home screen. From the dialog box that appears, you can set a new language, time zone, and the type of notifications you receive when using iCloud.com apps.

Via the Advanced option, you can reset your Photo Stream and remove all your photos from the iCloud servers but not remove any photos from your computer or iOS devices.

FIGURE 8-7

The iOS Atomic web browser can fool a website into thinking you're using a computer's browser

Access iCloud.com on an iOS device

For some reason, possibly to avoid confusion, Apple doesn't allow users to sign in to iCloud.com from the Safari browser on an iOS device. Fortunately, there is a way around the restriction: Just use a different browser on your iOS device; this fools the iCloud.com site into thinking you're signing in from a computer.

I use the Atomic web browser, although there are other options. Atomic allows you to set your iOS device to appear to a website as a desktop browser, including Safari and Internet Explorer (see Figure 8-7), which then allows you to sign in as normal and access some but not all the web-only features of iCloud. It's not a perfect solution, but it might come in handy as a last resort.

Use iCloud Documents

When Apple introduced iCloud Documents in spring 2012, many people thought they would be able to do away with their Dropbox and SkyDrive accounts in favor of the iCloud alternative. Although that's sometimes possible, iCloud Documents doesn't work the same way as most services that simply allow you to store files in an online folder for access on other computers and devices.

iCloud Documents is more of a syncing service for iOS and OS X apps than a storage service. Documents saved to iCloud are kept synced with the same app on all devices linked to the same iCloud account. Thus, iCloud Documents are treated as part of an app's contents, not as independent files as they would be on a traditional cloud storage service (or on a computer).

For example, if iCloud Documents is enabled for Pages on your iPad, as well as on your iPhone, any file you're editing on the iPad is available to Pages on the iPhone, and as you make changes to that document on any device those changes are kept synced to all the other devices as well — as long as they have Internet connections, of course. Pages on the Mac can also access these documents, with any changes made there synced to Pages on all your other devices. Pages on a Mac (running OS X Mountain Lion) can also save a new document to iCloud, making that document available to Pages on other devices. iCloud acts as a transit point, saving the latest version so it can relay it to other devices as needed.

But Pages' iCloud documents are available only to Pages, not other apps — even if they could open the file.

iCloud Documents-compatible apps are available in just two places: the iOS App Store and the Mac App Store. Apple requires developers who want to use iCloud Documents in their apps to sell those apps through Apple's app stores.

Many apps that support iCloud Documents have only iOS versions, such as GoodReader. Many have only OS X versions, such as Apple's own TextEdit and Preview. Some have both, such as IA Writer, Pages, Keynote, and Numbers.

Turn on iCloud Documents

As with most iCloud features, iCloud Documents is controlled from the Settings app on iOS devices and via the System Preferences app on a Mac. It is turned on by default when you set up an iCloud account on a computer or mobile device, and can be switched off and on at will. To work correctly, be sure to turn on iCloud Documents on all the devices you want to share files.

On a Mac:

1. Choose System Preferences and click iCloud to open the iCloud system preference.
2. Check the box next to Documents & Data (if it isn't checked already) to turn on iCloud Documents (see Figure 8-8).

On an iOS device:

1. Launch the Settings app.
2. Tap the iCloud label to open the iCloud pane.
3. Tap Documents & Data.
4. Set the Documents & Data setting to On (if it isn't on already) to turn on iCloud Documents.

FIGURE 8-8

Turning on iCloud Documents on a Mac

Share iCloud documents on a Mac

In OS X Mountain Lion apps that support iCloud Documents, there's a new location you can save files to and open them from: iCloud. After you launch an app that supports iCloud Documents, note the two tabs at the upper left of the window, as shown in Figure 8-9: ☁ iCloud and On My Mac.

Click ☁ iCloud to see existing iCloud documents for this app. Then:

○ Double-click a document as usual to open it. As you work on a document, changes are saved automatically to iCloud, though you can also choose File ➪ Save or press ⌘+S periodically to create new versions, a feature in OS X Mountain Lion that lets you revert to specific older versions of a document.

○ To create a new document, click New Document in the iCloud file list when first opening the app, or simply choose File ➪ New or press ⌘+N to open a new document window. Work on your document as normal. The first time you save it, or if you quit the app or close the window before saving the document, you'll be asked to provide a filename in a settings sheet that appears. That settings sheet also has the Where pop-up menu; choose ☁ iCloud to save it to iCloud, or choose a local disk or folder to save it on your Mac.

○ If you have a document stored locally on your Mac, you can send it to iCloud after opening it. Choose File ➪ Move To, then choose ☁ iCloud in the Where pop-up menu in the settings sheet that appears. Or just click the filename in the title bar and choose Move to iCloud in the pop-up menu that appears. You can also just drag a file from the Finder into the document window when set to ☁ iCloud, such as when first opening an app like Pages or Preview or saving a document for the first time.

Once you have saved a file to iCloud using an iCloud Documents-compatible app, you can access that file on all

FIGURE 8-9

iCloud documents in Pages on a Mac

devices connected to your iCloud account that use the same app.

TIP: You can find iCloud documents via the Mac's standard search functions. If you're searching from a Finder window, be sure to click the This Mac tab to find iCloud documents; a Spotlight search automatically looks in iCloud. And if you want to open such a document using an app other than the one you created it with, right-click or Control+click it and choose Open With from the contextual menu that appears and choose a different app from the one associated to its filename extension.

Share iCloud documents on an iOS device

The process for using iCloud Documents on an iOS device varies from app to app. Some — mainly Apple's Pages,

Keynote, and Numbers — simply automatically store all documents in iCloud if iCloud Documents is enabled for them. Others, such as GoodReader, present iCloud as if it were a folder along with its other storage locations.

How you enable iCloud Documents also varies. For Pages, Keynote, and Numbers, you go to their panes in the Settings app and set the Use iCloud switch to On. For GoodReader, the Use iCloud switch is accessed within the app, via its General settings pane (tap ✿ to open the Settings pop-over, then tap General Settings).

Transfer files via iCloud.com

iCloud documents from Apple's Pages, Keynote, and Number are available from iCloud.com for download to your computer; click the iWork button on the iCloud.com home screen to see available documents (see Figure 8-10),

FIGURE 8-10

You can transfer iCloud documents for Apple's Pages, Keynote, and Numbers apps at iCloud.com.

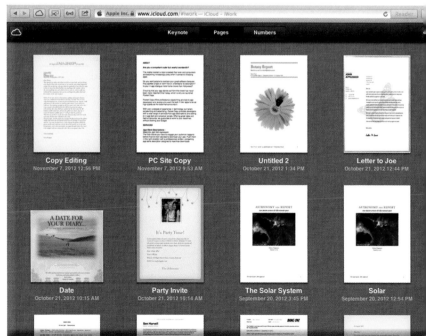

click the tab for the desired document type (Pages, Keynote, or Numbers), then click a document to have the Download button appear for that document.

To upload a file to iCloud.com to one of these apps, go to the app's pane, click the Settings button (✿) icon at the upper right of the window, choose Upload Document from the menu that appears, select the desired document on your computer in the dialog box that appears, and click Open.

Create folders for iCloud documents

Whether you use a Mac or iOS device to work with iCloud documents, you can create folders for them.

For Apple's Pages, Keynote, or Numbers in iOS:

1. Launch the desired app.
2. If the app opens to an existing file, tap the Documents button to view all your files.
3. Tap the Edit button.
4. The file icons begin to wobble, and you can now drag an icon onto another.
5. A new folder is created containing the two files.
6. Tap the title of the folder to edit its name, as Figure 8-11 shows. Tap outside the folder area when done to return to viewing all your shared files.
7. Drag more files to the folder if required.
8. Tap the Done button.

The process is similar in OS X for any app, not just Pages, Keynote, and Numbers:

1. Launch the desired app.
2. If the app opens to an existing file, choose File ⇨ New or press ⌘+N to open a new document window, and be sure to go to the ⌂ iCloud pane.
3. Whether you are in list view or icons view, drag an icon or filename onto another.
4. A new folder is created containing the two files.
5. Click the title of the folder to edit its name.
6. Drag more files to the folder if required.

FIGURE 8-11

An iCloud document folder in Pages for Mac, in icon view

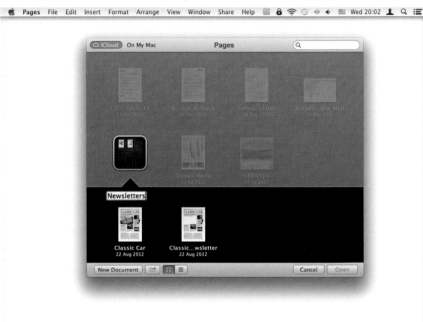

Use Cloud Storage Services

Several cloud storage services are available that allow computers and mobile devices to access the same files from one location via the Internet. The most popular are Box, Dropbox, Google Drive, and Microsoft SkyDrive, all of which have iOS apps and OS X apps available. Plus, many iOS apps directly support at least Box, Dropbox, and Google Drive, such as Quickoffice Pro, Documents to Go, Office^{2}HD, GoodReader, and CloudOn, so you can open and save cloud-stored documents from within them.

Apple's Pages, Keynote, and Numbers don't support cloud storage services other than Apple's own iCloud, but it does support a protocol called WebDAV that both Box and Dropbox support (for a monthly fee) that lets you open files from and export them to those services. It's not the same as being able to directly open and save files, but it's better than nothing.

To pull a file from a cloud storage service via WebDAV, tap the Add button (the + icon) in Pages, Keynote, or Numbers, then tap Copy from WebDAV in the pop-over that appears. Enter the WebDAV server for your storage service, as well as you username and password. Tap the desired document from the list that appear; it is copied to your iOS device. To save a document back to that cloud storage service, tap the Settings button ( ), then tap Copy to WebDAV in the pop-over that appears. Enter the WebDAV server for your storage service, as well as your username and password, then save the document. Note that the saved document will overwrite any document with the same name.

On the Mac, most of these services add plug-ins to the Finder when you install their OS X apps, so they appear to be hard drives attached to your Mac, which you access like any external hard drive, complete with the ability to drag files into and out of them, to rename files, and to add and delete folders. You can also go to their websites and sign in to access those documents.

Use File Sharing

With your photos, movies, and music all available on all your devices, it's time to look at the final piece of the puzzle: connecting all your devices together in your home for file sharing.

Access files remotely with Back to My Mac

The iCloud service on a Mac includes a feature called Back to My Mac, which lets you access files stored on other Macs wherever you have Internet access. Accessing files remotely can be unbelievably handy if you left an important document on your iMac at home but have your MacBook with you.

You enable Back to My Mac in the iCloud system preference by checking the Back to My Mac option. In the Sharing system preference, ensure that the File Sharing option is checked. You also want to make sure that the Finder is set to display Back to My Mac in Finder windows' Sidebars. To do so:

1. Click on your Mac's desktop to switch to the Finder.
2. Choose Finder ➪ Preferences to open the Finder Preferences dialog box.
3. Go to the Sidebar pane and make sure Back to My Mac is checked under the Shared section.
4. Close the Finder Preferences dialog box.

The target computer needs to be turned on and connected to the Internet for Back to My Mac to connect to it. It also needs to be signed into the same iCloud account as the computer you are trying to access it from.

All available Macs are shown in the Finder window's Sidebar, in the Shared section:

1. Click All to see the available Macs on the local network as well as found by Back to My Mac.
2. Click the name of the Mac you want to connect to.
3. Click the Connect As button.

FIGURE 8-12

Accessing files from another Mac via Back to My Mac in the Finder

4. Enter the username and password for the account of the Mac you want to connect to or, alternatively, click the Using an Apple ID radio button and enter your Apple ID and password.

5. Click the Connect button.

All the files stored on the target computer become visible in the Finder window, and you can move and edit them as you would any other file (see Figure 8-12).

Share files between Macs with AirDrop

AirDrop offers a convenient way to share files between two Macs running OS X Lion or later on the same Wi-Fi network. Unfortunately, only recent Mac models support AirDrop (typically, those built in 2010 or later). If you switch to the Finder and then open the Go menu, you will see the AirDrop menu option if your Mac supports AirDrop; if your Mac doesn't support AirDrop, the option does not appear.

AirDrop should also appear in a Finder window's Sidebar; if not, go to the Sidebar pane in the Finder Preferences dialog box, as explained earlier in this chapter, and check the AirDrop option.

FIGURE 8-13

Sharing files via AirDrop

Click AirDrop in a Finder window's Sidebar or choose Go ⇨ AirDrop in the Finder to scan for other AirDrop-compatible Macs on the network.

When it is active, it will scan for Macs using AirDrop nearby that have file sharing enabled in the Sharing system preference. Any such Macs will appear in the Finder window. You can then drag files onto those Macs' icons, and their users will get a prompt asking whether to accept the file you are transferring.

Share files between computers and iOS devices

There are a bunch of so-called air-sharing apps in the App Store that let your iOS device connect to your Mac or PC over a Wi-Fi connection so you can transfer files between them. Because iOS has no general file system where you store files for any app to access, files transferred to iOS this way are stored in the air-sharing app itself. You then use the Open In feature in iOS to transfer the file to an app where you can view or work with it: Tap and hold the file name or icon until the Open In pop-over appears, then select the app to open the file in). You also use Open In to get files to the air-sharing app from another iOS app. Of course, this only works with apps that use Open In.

The best app for air-sharing is the $5 GoodReader from Good.iWare (there are separate iPad and iPhone/iPod Touch versions), and it does much more than share files. It's a Swiss Army knife kind of app, providing a central file store, letting you transfer files to and from cloud services, letting to transfer files to and from computers, and letting you annotate PDF files.

In its Connect to Server section, tap Add to set up file sharing with your Mac or PC; Macs are called AFP servers and PCs are called SMB servers. You'll need the computer's IP address on the network, as well as any username and

FIGURE 8-14

GoodReader can transfer files between iOS devices and computers.

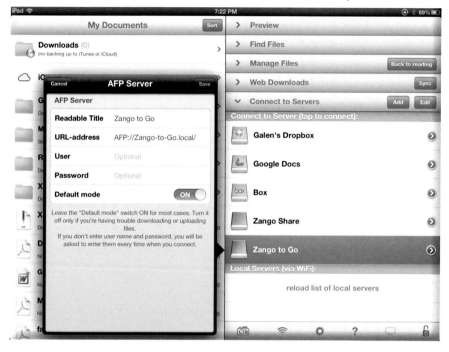

password required for signing in. You get a Mac's IP address in the Sharing system preference by selecting File Sharing. You get a PC's IP address by clicking the Start menu and entering **cmd** in the search field. Click the Command Prompt shortcut in the search results, then type **ipconfig** and press Enter in the window that appears. The IP address will be listed along with other network data.

Once you set up the connection, you can save it for easy use later, as Figure 8-14 shows. Tap the desired computer and then browse its contents to select what you want to transfer to or from GoodReader. Use the Open In facility to move documents between other iOS apps and GoodReader.

Use Remote Disc to access another Mac's optical drive

Since the MacBook Air, Apple has shipped several Macs without a DVD or CD drive. With OS X now sold only as an Internet download, with more and more media bought through iTunes and other online stores, and with more and more software sold as online downloads such as through the Mac App Store, the need for such drives is diminishing. As physical discs become more and more old-fashioned, you can expect these drives to one day disappear from most computers.

But there are times you need such a drive to install software or access files you may have burned to disc. In those cases, you have two options:

- The first is to buy an external optical drive, such as Apple's $79 USB SuperDrive.
- The other option is to use Apple's Remote Disc feature in OS X. It costs you nothing, but requires that you have another Mac that has a CD or DVD drive and is a fairly recent model.

To use Remote Disc, the Mac with the optical drive has to be running at least OS X version 10.4.11.

You can also use Remote Disc to access an optical drive on a Windows computer if it's running Windows XP Service Pack 2 or later, Windows Vista, Windows 7, or Windows 8 and has Apple's DVD or CD Sharing Update 1.0 for Windows software installed (available at http://support.apple.com/kb/DL112).

You can access that other computer's optical drive only from a Mac without its own optical drive, such as the MacBook Air, MacBook Pro with Retina display, late-2012 iMac, and Mac Mini and Mac Mini Server models without an optical drive. The Remote Disc software is part of OS X on those Macs, so there's no need to run an application; it's automatic.

The Mac without an optical drive and the computer whose optical drive you want to use need to be on the same network. Here are the steps to set up another Mac's optical drive for sharing over the network:

1. On the Mac with the optical drive you want to access, launch System Preferences (choose ⇨ System

FIGURE 8-15

Enabling disc-sharing on a Mac in its Sharing system preference

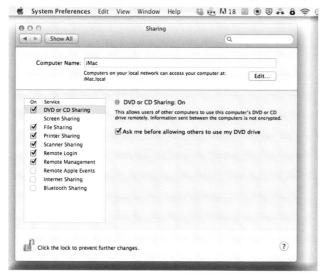

> Preferences or click the System Preferences icon on the
> Dock).
>
> 2. Click the Sharing icon to open the Sharing system
>   preference.
> 3. Select the check box next to DVD or CD Sharing and
>   close the Sharing system preference, as shown in
>   Figure 8-15.

The setup steps for a Windows PC's optical drive are
nearly same, but you also have to configure the Windows
firewall to allow access to that drive:

> 1. On the PC with the optical drive you want to access,
>   launch the Control Panel (via the Start menu on
>   Windows XP, Vista, and 7; via the Settings charm or
>   File Explorer in Windows 8).
> 2. Click on Hardware and Sound to get a list of
>   hardware-related control panels. Click DVD or CD
>   Sharing.
> 3. In the dialog box that appears, select the check box
>   next to Enable DVD or CD Sharing and close the
>   dialog box.

FIGURE 8-16

Accessing a disc on another computer from a disc-less Mac

4. In the Control Panel, click System and Security to get a list of security-related control panels. Under Windows Firewall, click the Allow a Program through the Windows Firewall link.

5. In the window that appears, click Change Settings and then Allow Another Program.

6. In the dialog box that appears, click Browse, then navigate to `C:\Program Files (X86)\DVD or CD Sharing`, select OSDAgent.exe, and click Open.

7. Click Add in the screen that appears.

8. In the confirmation window that appears, be sure that Home/Work is selected and click OK to enable sharing of the PC's optical drive.

Once you have enabled disc sharing on the remote computer, here's how you access it from your disc-less Mac:

1. On that remote computer's optical drive, insert the disc you want to share with your disc-less Mac.

2. On the Mac without an optical drive, switch to the Finder (click on the desktop or click the Finder icon in the Dock) and then choose File ⇨ New Finder Window or press ⌘+N.

3. In the Finder window's Sidebar, you should see Remote Disc. Click it.

4. The computer with the optical drive should now appear in the Finder window, as shown in Figure 8-16. Double-click it.
5. Click the Ask to Use button at the top of the window if required.
6. On the Mac or PC with the optical drive, accept the request (if required) to grant your other computer access to the drive.

NOTE: Some disc types and actions can't be used with Remote Disc:

- Copy-protected discs
- Audio CDs
- Operating system installation discs (both Windows and OS X)
- DVD movies
- CD or DVD burning

TIP: By purchasing apps from the Mac App Store, you can install them on as many as five Macs (using the same Apple ID) and reinstall and update as needed via the Internet — no installation disc required.

9

Do Even More with iCloud and AirPlay

AS CAPABLE AS ICLOUD AND AIRPLAY ARE IN THEIR OWN RIGHTS, IF you're willing to spend a little extra cash, you can create an even more connected environment or add features you thought were previously impossible. In previous chapters, I've mentioned many hardware add-ons and apps that enhance core capabilities such as watching TV and sharing information. But there's a whole raft of products and apps you can get to extend iCloud and AirPlay in unique ways. This chapter brings them under one roof.

Mac Mini Media Center

It may seem a little over the top to buy a Mac Mini solely as a media center but Apple's portable Mac is an ideal contender for living room use at a lower price than any other computer in the Mac line. Using the remote-control methods covered in Chapter 4, a Mac Mini can be the ideal partner for your TV, connected via an HDMI cable and controlled from an iOS device or other Mac.

Because the Mac Mini has built-in Wi-Fi and Ethernet, it can connect to your network easily and even share media from other computers. Unlike most set-top boxes, it has a suitably large hard drive to keep all your TV shows, movies, and music. You can also attach an external drive to the Mac Mini if you need more room and, of course, it can connect to a media server if you have one running on your network.

There are several apps that allow you to control a Mac as if it were a regular media-streaming box, including Plex and XBMC Media Center. These large, graphics-focused apps can help you quickly navigate your movies and music via your TV's screen and also allow you to install apps for viewing streaming content online.

Network

Although you may have all your devices and computers connected to the Wi-Fi router in your home wirelessly, there are other devices that you can throw in to the mix to add additional functionality.

Network drives

One option is to get a network drive that can be accessed by all your computers connected to the same network. Many companies make such drives, including Western Digital, Iomega, LaCie, Seagate, and Drobo. Multiple computers can use the network drive for sharing data, including movies and music. Most network drives come with their own server software to make the setup process easier. You can use the Mac's Time Machine backup software with most of them; for a Windows PC, such drives usually come with backup software.

Apple's Time Capsule ($500 for 3TB, $300 for 2TB) combines a wireless router and network drive so you can back up multiple computers over the network.

Wireless range extenders

If your home is too big for one wireless router or AirPort base station and you don't like the idea of running Ethernet cables throughout the house, a wireless range extender is likely your only option to ensure connectivity throughout your home. They're available from the major vendors of wireless routers, such as Netgear, D-Link, and Linksys. They pick up the wireless signal from your current router and then rebroadcast it, so you would locate an extender where the router's signal begins to diminish.

But before you run out and buy a product to boost your signal, consider a few factors. First, can you move your wireless router to a more central location in your home instead? Second, did your router come standard from your broadband provider? If so, it's likely not the best device on the market, and you should think about replacing it with a router that has a more powerful radio that could cover your home. Third, if you have Ethernet cables running to other locations in the home, you could attach a wireless router there (be sure to turn off DHCP via its settings) and use that as an extender — you'll get better speed if that relay router is connected to the main router via Ethernet than you'll get from a wireless extender connected over Wi-Fi.

Powerline networking

If you struggle to maintain a decent Wi-Fi connection throughout your home, you might want to look into the powerline networking options on the market. This technology uses your electrical wiring as network cables. Netgear and Devolo both offer such products, and I've used products from both to run a connection between my office and living room. But note that the transmission speed over powerline networks can vary dramatically, so be sure you can return powerline gear if it doesn't work well over your wiring.

Printers

iOS devices can print over Wi-Fi to printers that support Apple's AirPrint protocol, usually through the Share button (⤴) but sometimes through a button like Settings (⚙ or 🔧), as Figure 9-1 shows. Hewlett-Packard and Canon both sell printers that support AirPrint. But you don't have to get a new printer to use AirPrint.

Lantronix makes the xPrintServer series of devices that plug into your network and make almost any printer on it AirPrint-compatible. The $100 Home model supports two printers connected to your network via Ethernet or Wi-Fi, as well as to USB printers connected to its USB port (you can connect a USB hub to it if you want to AirPrint-enable multiple USB printers). The $150 Network model supports an unlimited number of network printers, but not USB models. The $200 Office model supports an unlimited number of network printers plus has a USB port, and it also has extra security features meant for business use.

FIGURE 9-1

If apps have a print capability and you have an AirPrint-enabled printer, you can print wirelessly from your iOS device.

Many routers let you connect USB printers to them, but they don't AirPrint-enable them, so only Macs and PCs can print to them. But some wireless routers such as the WNDR and R series from Netgear also have AirPrint support built-in, so network printers connected to them are enabled for AirPrint — as long as a Mac or PC is also on and running Netgear's free Genie software.

Several iOS apps let you print from iOS devices to printers connected to your network, but they don't use the Print option in most apps. Instead, then make you open or copy your document into the printing app, then print from there — an awkward process that works only with apps that support the Open In facility.

A better software option is to get Ecamm's $20 Printopia and run it on your Mac. It makes the Mac an AirPrint server that iOS apps "see" as an AirPrint printer; Printopia then relays the print job to a printer your Mac or PC can access directly or over the network. Collobos's $20 Fingerprint 2 for Windows works the same way for PCs.

Remote Control

In Chapter 4, I explained how to control your living room's home entertainment gear with iOS apps. But maybe you don't want to use your iOS device as a universal remote — that could interrupt your web surfing or game playing, for example. So you may want a separate universal remote, such as the $249 Logitech Harmony Touch. Like iOS-controlled remote apps, the Harmony Touch comes ready to handle common devices with preset functions and can quickly learn the commands for other devices, as well as let you build more complex command sets such as turning on the stereo, TV, and Blu-ray player at the same time.

But there are other forms of remote control beyond home entertainment gear.

Share screens with a remote Mac using Back to My Mac

As well as accessing files on your other computers remotely, you can view the screen of a remote computer using OS X's Back to My Mac capability covered in Chapter 8. This lets you run an app your current computer doesn't have but a remote Mac does.

You can also use screen sharing to avoid slow file transfers between Macs when using the remote file-sharing features of Back to My Mac. Let's say you're in a coffee bar with a poor Internet connection: Transferring a large file from your home iMac to your MacBook with Back to My Mac could take six grande lattes! Instead, because your home iMac is connected to a faster network (I assume), you can use the Screen Sharing feature of Back to My Mac to send the file to another location such as Dropbox or other cloud-based storage service to speed up things. Use the faster connection on your home iMac to upload the file and the faster servers of your cloud-storage service to download it to your MacBook via the crappy café Wi-Fi network. In principle, the process should be faster than simply dragging the file to your desktop from the Finder.

Screen Sharing also can help you with things like remotely shutting down a computer you left on accidentally (or after its backup is complete), sending e-mails from an account on your home computer not also on your current computer, and adjusting network settings.

If your Macs are set up for Back to My Mac, as explained in Chapter 8, here's how to use screen sharing:

1. Click All to see the available Macs on the local network as well as found by Back to My Mac.
2. Click the name of the Mac you want to connect to.
3. Click the Share Screen button.
4. Sign in with your username and password or Apple ID. (If another person is signed in to that Mac, you can still sign in to your own account without interrupting the other user.) The screen-sharing window appears, showing the desktop of your remote Mac (see Figure 9-2).

Here are some tips for using screen sharing:

○ Click the Automatically Send Clipboard Changes button at the top of the window to use Copy and Paste functions on the remote computer as if you were in front of it. For example, if you copy a passage of text on the remote computer, you can paste it into a document on the computer you are currently using and vice versa.

○ You can view the remote computer at full quality or adaptive quality depending on your Internet connection speed. The latter makes screen sharing more responsive at the expense of graphical clarity. Choose View ⇨ Adaptive Quality or View ⇨ Full Quality, as desired.

○ If the remote computer has an external display attached, you can choose to view both screens or pick one to control remotely, also in the View menu.

○ You can opt to fit the remote screen in a window or adjust the size of the window so that only a part of

---

FIGURE 9-2

Screen Sharing with Back to My Mac

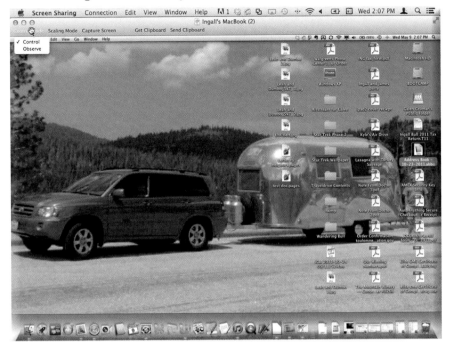

the remote screen is showing — just resize the window using the mouse or touchpad.

Control a Mac or PC from an iOS device

It's not just your Apple TV and home-entertainment gear that can be controlled by an iOS device. Your humble computer can also be accessed from the screen of an iPhone, iPad, or iPod Touch when using a local network or the Internet. For those who like to travel without a laptop, connecting remotely via an iOS device is an essential alternative to Back to My Mac.

Several apps allow you to control a PC or Mac from an iOS device, but I've found iTeleport to be the best option. The app requires installing a small piece of software called iTeleport Connect on your computer so the iOS device can recognize your

Mac or PC, but that's about it for the setup process. Once you've installed and set up iTeleport Connect, you should be ready to begin controlling your computer from the iTeleport app on your iOS device.

Simply select the computer you want to control and in a few seconds its display appears on your iOS device's screen. Your finger takes the place of a mouse or touchpad for selecting and dragging items, and you use iOS's onscreen keyboard to enter text as if you were at your desk. Although the performance isn't quite as fluid as when sitting in front of your computer, it's certainly usable for any quick tasks you forgot to do before leaving the house.

For accessing your computer on an iOS device via the web, you need to delve into darker arts, including setting up port forwarding on your router. This isn't quite as scary as it sounds, and iTeleport's support pages provide help.

For advanced users, there's also LogMeIn's expensive ($130) Ignition for controlling PCs and Macs remotely — it will even wake a sleeping Mac. Try the free "lite" version to help you decide if it's worth the cost.

FIGURE 9-3

Air Login on an iPhone

Another great tool for remotely accessing your Mac is Avatron Software's Air Login (see Figure 9-3), which I believe is the best looking and most useful app for the purpose. The app is free, but an annual usage subscription costs $15. Air Login works on both a local network and over the Internet and has extra features that make it truly stand out.

First, its interface is well designed and allows you to swipe across a view of all your available computers. When you connect to a Mac, the local menu bar feature makes a real difference: Instead of showing the normally tiny version of the menu bar on the remote Mac, Air Login adds a replacement to your iOS device's screen so you can quickly access menu items without performing the often fiddly process of clicking menus on the remote computer with the pointer.

Second, Air Login has a view called App Grid (see Figure 9-4) that shows all open applications on the remote computer

FIGURE 9-4

Air Login's App Grid view of apps on a remote-controlled Mac

so you don't have to launch the application switcher on the remote Mac or try to jump between apps using the dock which can get confusing, especially if you're using full-screen apps.

Finally — and arguably the best feature of Air Login — is that it doesn't require knowing anything about networking to set up. Simply create an account and you're good to go without worrying about firewalls and other common issues. Air Login is free for local network use and you can pay in the app to enable remote access features over the Internet if you want.

In addition to accessing your own Windows desktop over the network, you can run Windows via an Internet-based cloud service.

Through its free iOS app, the CloudOn service lets you run a Windows environment and Office apps over the Internet, from OnLive's servers. The CloudOn service is currently free, though the company may charge a subscription fee in the future.

FIGURE 9-5

CloudOn lets you access Microsoft Office via an Internet connection.

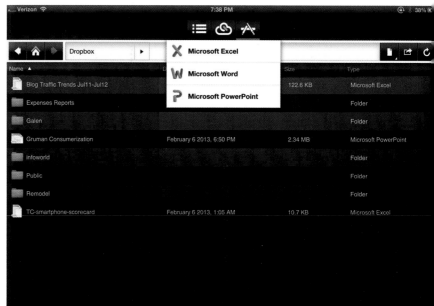

Once you connect and sign in, you get the Windows desktop and the Office apps (Word, Excel, and PowerPoint), as shown in Figures 9-5 and 9-6, which support basic gestures since you won't have a mouse with you, as well as the iPad's onscreen keyboard. (Sorry, no printing via AirPrint.) CloudOn lets you read and write documents stored on your iPad, as well as in the Box, Dropbox, Google Drive, and Microsoft SkyDrive cloud storage services.

To run Windows effectively, you need a connection of at least 1Mbps, which is what you get over a basic DSL connection and a Wi-Fi network. This means access over a cellular network will be painfully slow. To run games, you'll need a faster connection to keep up with the complex graphics as they change.

Keep in mind that apps such as Google Quickoffice and Apple iWork work with Office files very nicely, and cloud storage services such as Dropbox and Box are all that most

FIGURE 9-6

Using Microsoft PowerPoint via CloudOn

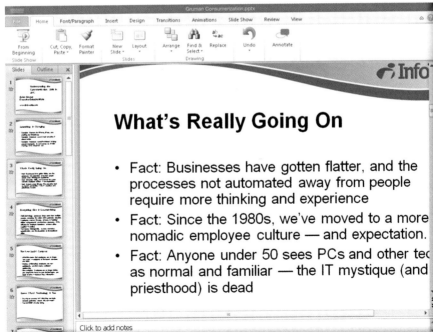

people need to work with Office documents. But CloudOn is very handy when you need a more sophisticated feature available only in Microsoft Office or a technology like ActiveX or Flash available only in Windows.

Control cameras with an iOS device

Your iOS devices are also capable of controlling creative tools like cameras and camcorders with clever apps that give you full remote control when you can't shoot and control a shot at the same time.

The $300 GoPro HD Hero3 video camera, for example, has built-in Wi-Fi that allows you to connect to it from your iOS device and take photos or shoot videos remotely. You can see a live video preview from the camera on your iOS device and play back clips you recorded.

Similarly, DSLR camera users will benefit from a free app called Triggertrap (see Figure 9-7) that works as a remote that triggers the camera shutter. Connected with a dongle and your standard camera connection cable, Triggertrap supports

FIGURE 9-7

The Triggertrap app

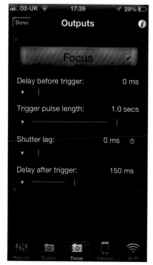

more than 300 camera types and adds features such as time-lapse control. With the $2 Triggercam version, the real fun starts when the device and app harness the iPhone's features to provide unique ways of triggering your camera such as facial recognition, shock and vibration sensing, sound sensing, and motion detection. I don't pretend to know the ins and outs of high-end photography, but I'm prepared to bet that building GPS functionality into triggering your camera is something that photographers would enjoy. This basically means you can apply clever shooting techniques for standard photography or time lapse by setting your camera to trigger every time it moves a certain distance. That's got to be good!

Smart Watch

The "next big thing" in iOS accessories appears to be the Bluetooth watch. The $150 Pebble, the most high-profile watch of this variety, links to your iOS device via Bluetooth, allowing you to see at a glance any alerts that may pop up without digging your device out of your pocket or bag. If you receive a text, the message is displayed on the screen. Receive an incoming call, and the caller's information appears on your wrist. The watch can control music playback on your device, be used as a golf rangefinder (whatever that might be) and, with an API available for developers, is set to gain many more features over time.

The Pebble already offers a range of apps that can be downloaded to the device to perform tasks as simple as changing the style of the watch face on its display or as complex as tracking a run or a cycle ride.

The Pebble isn't the only so-called smart watch available for iOS. There's also the $389 I'm Watch.

Home Automation

Although an expensive technology, home-automation technology can make the remote-controlled home dreams of Hollywood sci-fi movies a reality. To do home automation,

FIGURE 9-8

Control the lights from your iPhone, seriously.

you need the remote-controlled gear and the companion iOS apps — and sometimes a specialist to make it all work together.

But you can start small, such as with the smart-looking, $250 Nest thermostat, which learns your comings and goings to figure out when to heat your home and lets you monitor and control it via an iOS device. Heatmiser makes a similar series of more traditionally styled devices for £137 and up, but they require a Windows PC to set up.

Then there are remote-controllable lighting products, such as the incredibly cool Philips Hue bulbs and bridge ($238 for the starter pack, then $99 per additional bulb) that offer an extraordinary level of control over your home lighting. Not only can you turn off and on the lights (how 21st century!), you can create lighting themes and schedules with a simple touch of your iOS device's screen, as Figure 9-8 shows. You can even create light settings based on your favorite photos. Madness!

As well as providing these wild options, the Hue bulbs can be controlled from anywhere with an Internet connection so you can create the illusion of being at home even if you're on the other side of the world.

Similarly, blinds provided by companies like Loxone can be controlled by switch, automated and, you guessed it, via an iOS device.

Wireless CCTV

Adding video monitoring via closed-circuit TVs (CCTVs) to your network can be as James Bond or as paranoid as you want it to be. For ease, my personal favorite is the $335 Netgear VueZone Wire-Free Video Monitoring System that, as the name implies, is truly wireless. Unlike webcams and the like, this kit doesn't need software to set up, just a broadband connection and a free port on your router. Connect the base station, place the cameras, and you're up and running. Neither of the included two battery-powered cameras require cables (they work wirelessly with the base station), and you can place them in all sorts of places, including shelves, tables, or stuck on walls.

You can access live video from the cameras via your iPad, iPhone, iPod Touch, PC, or Mac by connecting to a dedicated website and — this is the really cool bit — pan and zoom the cameras while you watch. You can log in and view the feed from your cameras wherever you have Internet access on your iOS devices or computer. Unfortunately, the cameras in this kit don't offer a night-vision option, so they won't be ideal for monitoring outside your home in the dark. But for mundane tasks (like my checking on my cat while I'm away!), you really can't go wrong.

Meat Thermometer

The $100 iGrill from iDevices is a cooking thermometer that connects to an app (see Figure 9-9) on your iOS device via Bluetooth. Rather than hover around the grill to make sure your meat doesn't burn, you can spend time away from the heat enjoying yourself with your guests, safe in the knowledge that you can check the internal temperature of your food from your iPhone, iPad, or iPod Touch. With the

FIGURE 9-9

Barbecuing? There's even an app for that: the iGrill app for the iGrill thermometer.

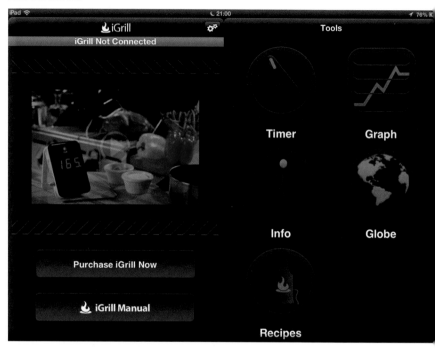

option to use two temperature probes, the iGrill can cater for more than just one menu item and, if you're really happy with what you're cooking, you can share information about your food to Facebook from the app.

Fitness Gear

The extra pounds you put on over the holidays don't escape the attention of your iOS devices, especially with so many fitness products available for computer and mobile platforms.

The flagship offering is, of course, the Nike + Sport Kit system that connects to your iOS devices and allows you to monitor your jogging and helps motivate you with a "power song" to help you push through the pain barrier. Modern iOS devices and larger iPods are ready to go with Nike+, but older devices need to use the Nike+ sensor attached to a shoe to chart your exercise. As you run, you get voice feedback on how you're doing, how far you've run, and, when you're finished, a full report to let you know if you're as fit as a fiddle or a flabby failure. You can sync the data to your www.nikeplus.com account to chart your progress and determine whether you're getting fitter or need to work out harder. You can even interact with and challenge other runners from around the world.

The $190 Nike + FuelBand does much the same job as the Nike + Sport Kit with a newer iPod or iPhone, but it also tracks your runs and your movements throughout the day. The wristband offers a clean LED display, doesn't look too ridiculous to wear on a day-to-day basis, and syncs wirelessly with your iOS device to provide detailed results. Throughout the day, lights on the band change from red to green, with the latter indicating that you've hit your fitness goal. At the end of the day, you can plug the band directly into your Mac via an available USB port to sync your data and further monitor your activity.

$159 Withings Wi-Fi Body Scale connects to your wireless network and sends information about your weight, muscle, and body mass index to an online account to help you track your development. You can also view your results via an app on iOS devices. The clever scale not only looks good but can figure out which person is using it, so you can add an account for each member of your household and challenge one another to a weight loss battle.

Likewise, the $130 Withings Smart Blood Pressure Monitor measures your blood pressure and provides a readout on your iOS device's screen.

iPad Headrest Mount

For long car journeys, an iPad can be the perfect tool to calm even the rowdiest toddlers with a Disney movie or a child-friendly game. The danger, of course, is that the iPad doesn't stay in their tiny grasp for the entire journey.

Enter the $70 Gripdaddy headrest mount that offers a fairly convenient way to attach an iPad to a car headrest so little ones can see the screen but not pick up the iPad. Put on your kids' favorite movie and drive in peace without the inevitable "are we there yet" from the back seat.

GarageBand

 Apple's $5 GarageBand app is one of the finest pieces of music software available for the iPad. Since its launch, it has been updated to include multi-user features so a group of people can play individual instruments together using multiple devices (see Figure 9-10).

The band leader in the group receives all the individual tracks on their device so they can edit the recordings into a finished song. The band leader can also set the key and time

FIGURE 9-10

GarageBand lets you play music with other iOS users

signature and all connected devices sync to those settings to make sure everything is in tune time.

GarageBand projects can also be sent to iCloud to edit them on multiple devices, and thanks to iCloud Documents syncing (see Chapter 8), they always remain up-to-date. You can even send projects created on an iPad to GarageBand for Mac or to Apple's advanced music production tool, Logic.

iA Writer

As much as I love Apple's Pages for crafting documents on all my devices, for simply writing I turn to iA Writer (see Figure 9-11). iA Writer offers a clean and unobtrusive interface with only essential tools like word count and auto-correction — plus iCloud Documents syncing. Available for iOS ($5) and OS X ($10), iA Writer is the ideal choice when it's all about the words and not the fancy graphics.

FIGURE 9-11

iA Writer for iPad

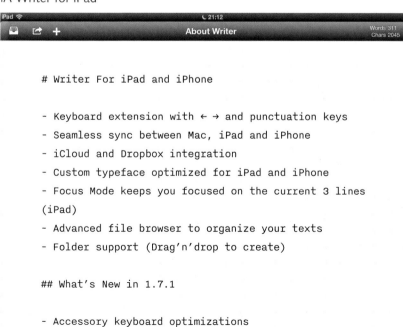

FIGURE 9-12

Apple's Cards app

E-cards

Sending postcards while you're on vacation is such an outdated idea. With Apple's Cards app (see Figure 9-12), you can snap a photo and have it sent as a e-card to friends and family back home. With a number of themes to choose from as well as photo manipulation and custom messages, the app is free but you pay $5 to have the card printed and sent.

A word of warning from my personal experience with this app: Almost every time I have sent cards from Cards while on vacation, I've arrived home before they have been delivered. So it's best to use Cards right at the start of your holiday unless you don't mind your friends and relatives having to wait around to hear about your trip.

Memo Sticky Notes

 With Post It notes going the way of pen and paper, stickies have become prevalent on computers, so it's nice to see that the digital equivalent is continuing to keep pace with evolutions in technology. The $2 Memo Sticky Notes by Bloop is a cute little app for OS X and iOS that allows you to create notes on any device and sync them to all your other devices via iCloud. There are separate versions for iPads and for iPhones and iPod Touches.

Ridiculous Luxuries

For those who haven't had enough of expensive yet ultimately useless gadgets to use with their iOS devices, how about the $300 Parrot AR Drone? It's a quadricopter (four-fan helicopter) controlled by your iPhone or iPad that has a built-in camera to snap photos and record video. Usable indoors and out, the Parrot AR Drone can let you play racing games to play against friends who also own such a contraption.

Then there's a $600 pair of Oakley Airwave GPS Enabled Goggles for the skier who has everything, including money to burn. This fancy eyewear provides a head's-up display that pulls GPS data from your iPhone and measures speed, jumps, and tells you where your friends are. You can even control music playback and make calls. These goggles are a true luxury item that syncs beautifully with your iPhone.

appendix

Apple TV Tips and Tricks

THE APPLE TV IS REALLY EASY TO USE: USE THE REMOTE CONTROL to move to a button for whatever media you want to access — Movies, TV Shows, Podcasts, Music, Computers, Hulu Plus, Netflix, or whatever, as well as Settings — then press the center button (called Enter or Select) to open that service's offerings. Navigate and open content offerings the same way, as well as menu options and settings, which if available appear at the right side of the screen. Click Menu to go back up a level in that navigation, such as to the previous menu level or to the previous content options and ultimately the Home screen.

TIP: Press and hold the Menu button while playing content to jump directly back to the Apple TV's Home screen.

It's an anachronistically simple interface in this age of remotes with dozens of buttons. Figure A-1 shows the Apple TV's Home screen, which shows content options for the currently selected library or store at the top. Figure A-2 shows the menu options for, in this case, genre options for the iTunes Store's movie selections.

FIGURE A-1

The Apple TV's Home screen, showing available movie content at the top

The Genre menu options for iTunes Store movies

But there are a few tricks to using the Apple TV that aren't obvious from its simple interface. This appendix walks you through them.

Get More While Watching Movies and TV Shows

When you're watching a video, press the up or down button on the Apple remote to get the scrub bar that shows you how far along you are in your video, as Figure A-3 shows. The scrub bar will fade away after a few second, or press either button to dismiss it.

When you're going through the available titles for movies and TV shows from the iTunes Store, Netflix, or other services, you see options for more information in the information screen for the specific show. But you won't see a chapter list for movies. Nor will you see them for your own iTunes library's movies, even if they have chapter markers. (TV shows from the iTunes Store do not have chapter markers, though TV shows you import into your iTunes library may, depending on how you import them.)

FIGURE A-3

The scrub bar shows your current position in a video.

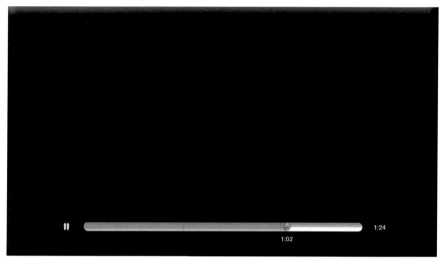

So how do move among chapters in a movie? The answer: Press and hold the center button for a few seconds to open the Chapters screen shown in Figure A-4. Then navigate to the chapter you want. If it's a commercial movie from the iTunes Store, you'll see visual chapter markers, as Figure A-4 shows. Otherwise, you'll likely see just a text list.

FIGURE A-4

The Chapters screen in an iTunes Store movie

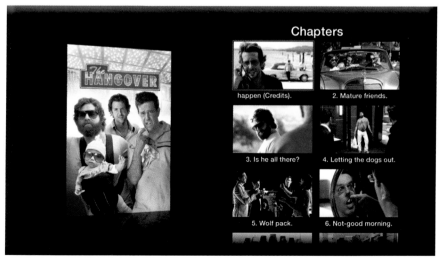

For most videos — from the iTunes Store or your iTunes library — you can also change the audio options by scrolling all the way to the top, then horizontally to the Audio tab. Select it to get the Audio screen of available audio options for the current movie, if there are any. Likewise, the Closed Captions tab appears if the video has the option to display captioned dialog; select it to open the Closed Captions screen. The Speakers screen, also available through a tab at the very top, lets you switch the audio to other AirPlay devices without going into the Settings screen.

When watching movies on Netflix or other streaming services, pressing and holding the center button may also open a screen with options, such as enabling subtitles or changing the active AirPlay speakers, as Figure A-5 shows. Test the services you use to see what additional controls they provide using this technique.

TIP: If you decide not to change chapters or other options, press and hold the center button for a second or two to resume the movie where you left off.

FIGURE A-5

The dialog box of options for a song

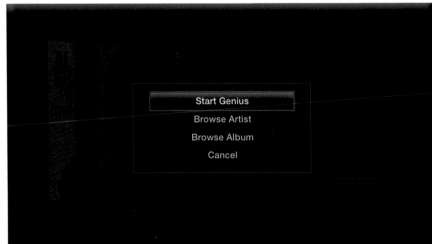

Get More While Listening to Music and Podcasts

That press-and-hold trick also works for music and podcasts. For music, you get a dialog box (shown in Figure A-5) with options such as to browse the album, browse the artist, open the Genius feature to find music similar to the current song, see what song will play next (in your shuffle, album, or playlist) and change the AirPlay speakers in use. If you press and hold the center button on a song in a playlist, album list, or other list, you get a dialog box with options to play the song now, play it next, open the Genius feature, show what will play next, add the song to the Up Next list, or browse the artist.

For podcasts, you just get the option to change the AirPlay speakers in use when pressing and holding the center button while a podcast is playing. But when you're viewing a list of podcast episodes, pressing and holding the center button opens a dialog box where you can mark the episode as played or unplayed. Similar options are available in episode lists of TV shows.

Get More While Listening to Internet Radio Stations

When you find a radio station you like in the Radio screen (from the Home screen's Radio button), add it to your Favorite Stations list. To add the station, play it, and then press and hold the center button until the dialog box appears. Select Add Station to Favorites to add the station to the list. After you add the first radio station to your favorites, the Favorite Stations list appears near the top of the Radio screen, as Figure A-6 shows. From here, you can quickly select one of your favorite stations.

Your Apple TV has an impressive list of Internet radio stations, but you may also want to listen to stations that don't appear on the list. You can't do this directly on your Apple TV

The Radio screen, with the Favorites section at top

— but if you have a computer, you can play the station easily using iTunes. You can then send the output to your Apple TV via AirPlay, so you have the station playing on the Apple TV. Here's how to open another radio station in iTunes:

1. Find the station's URL. The easiest way is to go to the station's website and look for the link.
2. Copy the URL. For example, right-click or Control+click the link, and then choose Copy on the contextual menu that appears.
3. Open iTunes or switch to it.
4. In iTunes, choose Advanced ⇨ Open Stream. The Open Stream dialog box appears.
5. Type or paste the URL for the radio station and then click OK (or press Enter or Return). iTunes tunes into the radio station, which starts playing. You can control playback of the radio station using the standard iTunes playback controls.
6. Click the AirPlay button in the lower-right corner of the iTunes window and choose your Apple TV from the pop-up menu that appears. iTunes starts streaming the radio station to the Apple TV.

TIP: The same technique works to play podcasts not listed on the Apple TV's Podcasts screen and not in your iTunes library's subscribed podcasts. Just use a podcast's URL instead of an Internet radio station's.

Set Up and Use a Remote Control

Your Apple TV comes with a sleek remote control that enables you to navigate its user interface easily. The Apple Remote usually needs no further maintenance than the occasional battery replacement. However, you can also use your preferred universal remote to control your Apple TV, which might give you dedicated buttons for actions, such as skipping ahead or back, that the Apple Remote doesn't offer. As explained in Chapter 3 for audio and Chapter 4 for video, you can also turn your iPhone, iPod Touch, or iPad into a remote, and control your Apple TV from a device that you always have with you.

Using a different remote offers several advantages:

- **Simplicity.** You can control your Apple TV with the same remote you use for other devices, so you don't have to switch remotes in midstream.
- **Easier control.** You can teach your Apple TV to respond to buttons beyond the six on the Apple Remote. Extra buttons can make playback easier. For example, you can dedicate a button to skip ahead or return to the beginning of an item.
- **Handiness.** If you have large hands, you may find a larger remote easier to use — even if it has many more buttons.

The Apple TV is pretty compatible with other remotes and works with many different kinds. If you already have a universal remote, chances are that you can get the Apple TV to respond to it. Similarly, if you already have an extra remote, it's worth trying that remote before buying a new one. If you want to use a universal remote, make sure it has a free device setting. If you choose a single-device remote, use one that you're not using with any other device.

NOTE: Another option is to use an existing remote that has extra buttons you're not using for your current remote-control setup. You can map those buttons to control both your existing devices and your Apple TV from the same remote control — but it may mean using awkwardly placed or little-used buttons on the remote for the Apple TV.

Once you have your remote, follow these steps to set it up with your Apple TV:

1. From the Home screen, select Settings. The Settings screen appears.
2. Select General. The General screen appears.
3. Select Remotes. The Remotes screen appears, as shown in Figure A-7.
4. If you're adding a universal remote, choose an unused setting. If you're setting up a single-purpose remote that will be dedicated to the Apple TV, you don't need to change anything.
5. Select Learn Remote. The first Learn Remote screen appears.

FIGURE A-7

The Remotes screen is where you begin configuring your Apple TV to work with a third-party remote.

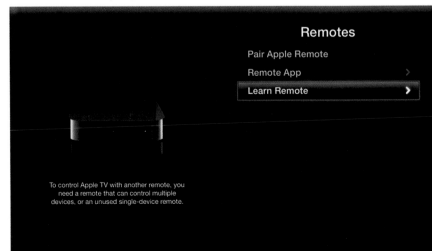

FIGURE A-8

The second Learn Remote screen is where you assign Apple TV remote functions to buttons on a third-party remote.

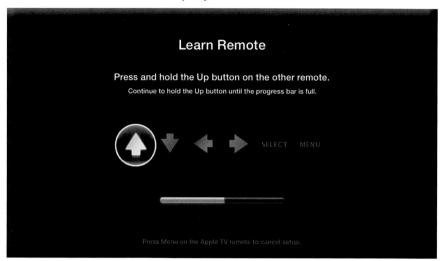

6. Using your Apple Remote, select Start. The second Learn Remote screen appears, shown in Figure A-8.

7. Press and hold the up button on the third-party remote until the blue progress bar on the Apple TV advances all the way to the right.

8. Follow the training routine until you have taught your Apple TV all the standard buttons. The Remote Control Name screen then appears.

9. Type the name you want to give the remote.

10. Select Submit. The Setup Complete screen appears. If you're done setting up the remote, select OK and skip the remaining steps.

11. If you want to set up extra buttons on the remote to control playback, select Set Up Playback Buttons. The Learn Remote screen then appears, as shown in Figure A-9.

12. Press and hold the Play button on the third-party remote until the blue progress bar on the Apple TV advances all the way to the right.

FIGURE A-9

The Learn Remote screen when setting up additional playback buttons

13. Continue the training process by pressing and holding each button until you have configured all that you want to use for playback on your Apple TV.

14. When you reach the end of the training, the Remotes screen appears again, and now includes the remote that you added in the Other Remotes list. Press the Menu button to return to the General screen, and then press it again to return to the Home screen.

NOTE: In Step 13, if you press a button you've already assigned to a different function, the Apple TV displays the Button Already Learned screen as a warning. Select Try Again to go back and assign another button. When on the screen for assigning buttons, you can press the left button to go back to an earlier button in the sequence and reassigning buttons.

Make the Apple TV Play More than Apple Wants

If you want to get even more out of your Apple TV than is possible with the apps you've seen so far in this book, you can jail-break your Apple TV and install unapproved third-party software. For example, you can install the popular aTV Flash software to add capabilities ranging from playing DVDs and other media formats the Apple TV doesn't natively support to surfing the web and keeping up with blogs.

Out of the box, the Apple TV's software contains protective features that keep it within the ecosystem that Apple designed and limit it to running software approved by Apple. This ecosystem is called a *walled garden* — a safe area protected from the wilds of the Internet. *Jail-breaking* involves installing a customized version of iOS that removes the protective features, allowing the Apple TV to go outside the walled garden.

This book doesn't show you how to jail-break your Apple TV, but you can easily find instructions on the Internet. The technology changes rapidly, so before attempting a jail-break, double-check that the instructions apply to the Apple TV model and version of iOS that you are using. And note that there's a risk you may damage your Apple TV beyond repair.

If you jail-break your Apple TV, you may well want to install the $30 aTV Flash a suite from FireCore (http://firecore.com) or try out any of the free alternatives. It allows you to supercharge your Apple TV in several ways, including:

- ▶ **Installing extra software.** You can customize your Apple TV by choosing which apps and packages to install (see Figure A-10).
- ▶ **Playing other media formats, including DVDs**. aTV Flash includes XBMC Media Center, as shown in Figure A-11, which offers information and entertainment ranging from weather forecasts and Internet radio to music and video playback from your network-attached storage (NAS) device. XBMC can even play DVD files that you've copied from physical discs.
- ▶ **Surfing the web.** The Browser app enables you to browse the Web without leaving your Apple TV. Typing URLs on the onscreen keyboard is cumbersome, but you can easily follow links and bookmark pages to

return to later. Or simply use a Bluetooth keyboard instead.

Jail-breaking an Apple TV enables you to install apps and packages to add extra features.

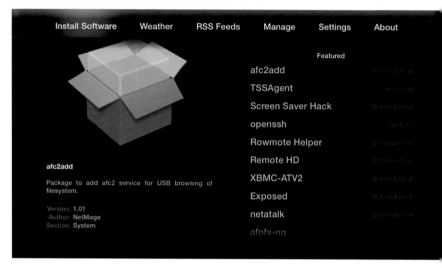

The XBMC Media Center adds further entertainment options to your Apple TV and even provides a weather forecast

○ **Keeping up with blogs and websites.** You can read RSS feeds directly on your Apple TV, which is great for staying up to date with your favorite sources of information.

○ **Last.fm.** This service provides Internet radio that you can customize with your personal stations.

index